COOM CONSUME COMPLY

ALSO BY STEVEN FRANSSEN:

Torturing The Villagers

Fire In The Pines

Dead West Walking

Make Self-Knowledge Great Again

COOM CONSUME COMPLY

STEVEN FRANSSEN

stevenfranssen.com

twitter.com/stevefranssen

youtube.com/c/stevenfranssen

To everyone who trusts the plan.

Preface

As it was with *Torturing The Villagers*, this book has no table of contents. *Coom Consume Comply* was written in less than six weeks and I began writing it the day after *Torturing* published. I did this slightly as a flex but mostly because there was a lot I didn't get around to saying in *Torturing*. You can compare these two books to a pair of detectives or gamer brothers. They're supposed to complement one another.

This book is concerned with the operating ethos foisted upon modern man: coom, consume, comply. Cooming is for simps. One of the best reviews for my last book was, "This book helped me stop cooming." I hope this one will help you, too. Anyone familiar with my social media output knows I am no friend of rampant consumerism. Here I tackle some of the more seductive aspects of New America's shopping mall extravaganza. Lastly, enforcing our self-effacement and materialistic gluttony is the Leviathan: a rampaging terror beast into whose jaws our civic leaders shovel the unborn. I heckle the Beast some and give women a hard time. If you're into that, you're going to love this book!

-Steven Franssen
December, 2019

Crypto Kultura

"Crypto libertarian visionaries" pursue their "futuristic decentralized" vision of society because they're conflict-averse and can't deal with people problems. These people are not going to save the world with one more decentralized app on the blockchain. That's just a cope for being a sperg with coombrain.

Bill Gates is the godfather of all this spergery. There's no denying that funding the invention of water cleaning and waste processing machines to be deployed on a mass scale in Africa would lead to good in the world. But this is a rich man's cope for A) having crappy political beliefs and B) for being utterly regulated out of any efficaciousness in the United States. There are relatively few regulations to contend with in Africa. That's why most developed nations treat it as their petri dish for experimentations. Bill Gates' crappy politics come from a number of factors, including the globo-homo system that made him one of the wealthiest people in the world. He has no incentives to do anything of substance for Americans. Sure, he provides a few of them jobs. He outsources a lot of their jobs to India and China. He's making money, right? There's no opportunity cost to what he's doing and of course, someone would just step right in and do what he's doing if he wasn't doing it. That's what libertarians would have us believe. Bill Gates could spend the rest of his fortune fighting for Americans but that would probably lead to his assassination because it violates some blood oath he took. Bill Gates gets to exist as a moral evildoer, compared to absolute standards, because he satisfies the libertarian's requisite that he not actively increase the size of the state. He's pursuing market opportunities in Africa, after all! Global arbitrage. He's a victim of the state just like the rest of us!

2

Blockchain visionaries are a bit better because they can at least claim to be fighting the Federal Reserve. Yet, when I look at what they're doing, they're posting candlestick charts, bickering about the rival cryptocurrency, grandiosity poasting about the glories of their particular currency, or doing absolutely retarded shit like launching satellites into orbit or dicking around in the Third World. These aren't people who are equipping themselves to resolve the real, interpersonal problems at the forefront of the national conversation. Where is the blockchain app developer who is developing a system that will differentiate citizens from non-citizens? Where is the crypto millionaire who is pouring resources into the private effort to "Build The Wall" along America's southern border? Where is the "visionary" who is using their crypto fortune to put our people into political office? I don't see these people. Perhaps they exist. Reach out to me, if you're out there. Until then, I just see a bunch of interpersonally incompetent libertarian types creating a culture of soft, anarchic, and socially leftist self-indulgence around themselves. They made their fortunes in the bull run. Time to do shrooms in Denver and have a dance party at the Ethereum conference! Time to take on a 5-year lease on an apartment in Manhattan in order to glad-hand with other crypto enthusiasts while Middle America is hollowed out by mass legal migration.

Money is nice. Money is fun! It's the fuel for choices. I am not disparaging wealth-acquisition in and of itself. People who took the risk to invest in crypto and made their money thusly have no reason to fear envy from me. I'll be thrilled when the Federal Reserve is disbanded. But fortunes wasted on self-indulgence and pet projects are just more distractions put in the way of those of us who are engaged in *the argument*. I'd like more money. Who wouldn't? But I'm not going to pull myself out of the fight to engage in what boils down to a drug user's mindset on things: jailbreak the system from without. This is simply the eradication of boundaries masquerading as some noble cause that you can only understand if you engage in it yourself. This is stupid. You only defeat the Leviathan by confronting it and tearing it down, stone by stone. You can't wriggle your way around it by getting really high. No, the endorphin rush of watching your crypto fortune 10x is not actually an argument. Having a net effect on society means engaging the difficult conversations, not succumbing to the discomfort you provoke in others, and gently, kindly, ever-so-sweetly dislodging your political enemies from their positions of power (using your free speech, of course).

I get that everyone has their own thing. "Be a based and redpilled plumber" is more or less what I said in *Torturing The Villagers*. I have no problems with crypto-rich people. I have an address. Send me some money! I'm simply taking issue with the "visionary" ego some of these folks carry around with them. Just because you made a fuckton of money does not mean you are the person most prepared to spend that money. Melinda Gates is spending $1 billion USD on "advancing gender equality through the world". Bill Gates, in his wizard-like judiciousness, gave a large chunk of that money to her. Is he doing good in the world by "spending money"? Of course not. Same goes for crypto-libertarians who suddenly think they've got the solution to the world's problems because their couch cushion money 50x'ed on them. This is a world ruled by violence. Crypto-currency made it to its current standing because the Leviathan was slow to regulate against it. Tech is the only industry left relatively unregulated because the oligarchs want the technology to permanently subdue the middle class into serfdom. There will probably be no great

4

buckling of the Leviathan crashing under its own weight because the elite have amassed sufficient resources, technology, and cultural hegemony to simply institute, by force, their world order when the time is right. There's no dodging and weaving around this when a hyper-socialist "Congress" can simply institute the death sentence for anyone who holds Bitcoin and quell the subsequent insurrections with the Terminator style robots people like Bill Gates and Mark Zuckerberg have been developing for years and years now. I am more than happy to be proven wrong here.

Love In The Time Of Clown Era

Love these days is hard to find. The sexual market is skewed heavily toward women and alpha men. The thirst is real. I should write a whole book on love, relationships, and dating. The groundwork has already been laid with my subscription lecture series *The Road To Self-Knowledge*. Until I get around to writing that book, the lecture series is your best bet on my thoughts on dating.

I have helped many men find women. Women are trouble. They have their pick of the litter. They choose poorly. They go with their hearts when their hearts have been programmed against them via emotional propaganda in the mainstream media. I know I'm supposed to say "corporate media" here but until the public schools are disbanded, the mouth-breathers at the major networks will have unending amounts of test subjects for their bullshit. Women have been the primary test subject. Their boundaries are more pliable. They gravitate toward the most certain force in the room, especially when they come from weak fathers. The wealth of the generations has not been passed on but the entitlement has. This hits women hard and they get an overinflated sense of themselves. Besides, the entire Third World wants to screw them. They can get what they want. They will simply fork into other nations and other peoples. They are not disturbed by the conquering of Western Civilization by outside forces, not to the degree that men are. They don't quite share our existential dread and need for the fight to carry on while we muster our strength. Women aren't plugged into that. Nor would it be reasonable to expect them to be. They will go with the victors. So many of them already have. But the contest hasn't been decided yet. They're jumping the gun! They're going over early. Naughty, naughty!

I love the women that choose to remain with us, despite the odds. I'm whitepilled about our prospects. Some of them get the whitepill but none of them can carry the fight like the men can. There's a fatalistic streak in these women: a pride in the face of extinction. I love these women. They're a strange sort. Their fathers were stronger than the norm, much stronger. But in their lack of clarity they put their paranoia into their daughters, as well. When the landscape is filled with jackals and simps, the proper survival strategy for a woman is to run *fast*. Some of these women don't know when the fuck to slow down. They pick men who are *fast* like them and things veer out of control. The fast men pick better because they've existed in the role of hunters. Fast women should leave it to fast men to do the picking. The paranoia in these women, put there by their fathers, is a discerning eye for the bullshit of the world. The unfortunate thing is that the father's tenuous connection with the truth (from being constantly on-

6

guard from having existed through the ascendance of globohomo), makes these women flighty. I say *fast* because they *are* pursued but they also were failed by their fathers, who didn't branch them into networks where good men would snap them up, and so they have an insecurity streak in them. Taming one is a hell of a trick. They're stubborn as shit, especially when they're younger and in the heat of fertility. It's in their best interests to choose *our* neck of the woods and *slow down*. Getting them to see that is often difficult because they pursue intellectual existences in order to not be fouled up by the shit their fathers warned them about.

Empathizing with these women for a second, I recognize the sheer number of autists they perceive. Men who are not connected to the feminine because feminism wrecked their own mothers. It's a tough spot to be in for a *fast* woman. Autists will read this book. There will be men who never connect with the feminine who will be left on the outside looking in. I referred to them in my last book, *Torturing The Villagers*, by saying something to the effect of, "Not everyone is going to make it." I will provide as much as I can, in these pages on my platforms. The truth is that these women see just how many men can run *fast* because of their intellects but still ring hollow because of love deficits. Why put oneself into the computerized sperg mitts of an incompetent who, sure, may provide resources but can't fall in true love? Happens all the time. So many women dying in darkness. Flaming out. I'm no feminist. I am a father. I can't tolerate all this misery and all these missed connections. I call the *true kings* to me. Frankly, nobody else is doing it on this level. These *fast* women can't be tamed from the outside. I can only make my appeals. I know the way out of madness, desolation, desperation, isolation, and the death of potential. I know the path to the fulfillment of potential. I know the secrets of this thing "chemistry" that is so commonly referred to. I'll convey as much as I can over the Internet but it's a felt sense. I'll approximate it. We'll see who responds. We're sowing the seeds of true love here. Who will sprout up?

Very Stable Genius

No doubt, certain parties have put visibility roadblocks in my way. I watch our guys blow up on the scene with a bunch of follows coming their way only to be crushed under immediately by the algorithm. The Silicon Valley nubs want me to believe that I was stagnant only until recently and that when it plateaus-off again for me, it will be because I am not engaging at an ever-growing depth. These are their lies. This is how threatened they are. They don't want to share the advertising deals, the financing, the exposure, or the platforms. I am Dr. Phil's hidden nightmare. I don't experience it this way. I'm over here talking about love and trudging around the woods. I am a nightmare for all of the oligarchs, the gatekeepers.

I will be having a lot of fun when the levee breaks. If it does. I'm optimistic. Many people will come flocking in. Good people. We will accomplish a lot together. I have always said that I am playing for my 50's and 60's. I've been saying this for almost 10 years now, as I write this in late 2019. I think that's how long it will take, so I am patient. The biggest dissidents of the past few years have not wanted anything to do with me even though I've been making the arguments and observations they won't for a while to come, all with the composure and tenderness they have yet to learn. I used to get impatient about this but now I don't. I'm in a great spot. I long have been, just needed to appreciate it more. These things take time. I will spearhead or be *just* off-center of the thing that's coming. Hard to say. I keep looking for leaders. There are scant few. We'll change that, though. Some of my job, as I see it, is to convey as much of this as possible as soon as possible in a way that will not evoke panic *now* but be well-received in the future when the path is more paved. If I slow down in 20 years, I know enough to know when to get the fuck out of the way. The thing is, I don't think I will slow down. Trump's carrying the fight in his 70's. He's a rare one. So am I. You fuck with it if you degenerate, though. Respect what you have.

The Perfect Family Man

This man is handsome. Not too handsome, as that can be a double-edged sword. Look at his family, it's ideal! He has one son and one daughter. That's all he wants to have because that's what a marketing firm told him. "Keep it to two children so you look strong to your voting base but can also appeal to the other side of the aisle. We don't want anyone thinking you're taking more than your fair share." His donors pay for this personal branding strategy, to the tune of tens of thousands of dollars a year. They also pay for his teeth whitening. He's a winner! Did you know he served in the military?

Our guy is also a *value creator*. He's made jobs, you know? We're not going to get into the specifics. What you need to know is that he wears nice suits, classy wristwatches, and has a trophy wife. She's blonde. You don't need to scrutinize too closely to see if her hair is dyed blonde or if she has had Botox. That's mean. Stop being mean. She supports him dutifully. She's great at delegating around the house. She can tell the chef to whip something up. She can tell the maid to pick up that dirty shirt off the floor. She can tell the gardener to wet his back further with sweat in the midday sun. She is truly a throwback. You'd love to meet her, as would anyone. Her taste in cocktail dresses is unmatched.

When he was younger, our guy did some important things for society. He went to the right schools. Remember, he came from a hard-scrabble life. Nothing was handed to him. He had to struggle to get what he has. He's an American Success Story. There's nothing more inspiring than that. Imagine it, a man born to meager circumstances who pulls himself up by his bootstraps. Goes into the military, kills our enemies, comes back and gets put into an elite school that churns out global leaders, and then becomes a *jobs creator*. That's the way you do it. My favorite story of his time in the service is the one about his service dog, a German Shepherd named Yankee. America loves Yankee. He was a bomb-sniffing dog who got blown up. It was heart-breaking. He wasn't a *pet* but we love him anyway. He was a hero!

This may be a little controversial but the media is *terrified* to cover it because they don't want to send converts to our Perfect Family Man. We're gonna call him PFM from now on. The inside scoop is that he is teaming up with the people for who pay for his teeth whitening to do something unprecedented in American history: he is going to go from trailer park to trailer park, burning each of them down and flogging the people inside with bats as they run to escape the flames and save their children. Aren't you excited? I sure am. I'm actually higher up in his organization because I have been a good ambassador for the cause. If you want, we can send a care package including a lapel pin that states who we support, some bumper stickers that will "trigger" our enemies (I love using that term!), a baseball bat, and of course, three incendiary grenades so you can clear out any local trailer parks in your area. Join the PFM Team!

I can see you're *triggered*. Hold on a second while I gloat in delight at your confusion, anger, and malevolent obfuscation of the tremendous work we're doing. Our mutual audience needs to see me deftly handle this hysteria you're whipping up by calmly and confidently sticking to the talking points I learned from PFM training materials. Okay, here I go. There's a great, big misunderstanding about our burning down trailer parks, viciously clubbing anyone who escapes the flames, and high-fiving each other while the flames devour anyone stupid enough to be trapped inside the trailers. The fact remains that PFM and I, who are close friends, are committed to doing this *legally* because it is in America's best interests. Now, we understand how some people would want to restrict this. We're sympathetic. That's why we support the Burn People Less Act that reduces legal trailer park infernos by about 25%. Let's be real, to get this Act through Congress, we're probably going to have to settle for a 12% reduction.

We're not opposed to firebombing trailer parks on principle, that is the sickening bigotry of the Racists talking. They're racists. Remember how our political enemies promoted CIA Stooge A, CIA Stooge B, and CIA Stooge C? Yeah, those guys are racists. They're all bad. They want to shut down the trailer park hellfire program completely. That's not what America stands for and frankly, anyone who even momentarily thinks about a

11

moratorium on burning trailer parks to the ground and the survivors being clubbed to death should be ashamed of themselves. If you think back on history, not that long ago, there were persecuted people who had to live without their shacks being set alight by *job creators*. That was horrific. We don't want to put people through that again. America is a proposition nation where anyone can come here and be firebombed to death by PFM and our outstanding organization. We don't care if you're from Africa. We don't care if you are a Chinese student here to spy on American tech companies. We don't care if last year in your far-flung village there were corpses being dug up and danced with, triggering outbreaks of the plague. We want you to come to America, live in one of our trailer parks, and get firebombed in the good old American Way. After all, we hold these truths to be self-evident, that all men (this includes eunuchs who elect to butcher their own genitals) are created equal. Everyone gets to have incendiary grenades thrown onto the roofs of their trailers and then surprise-attacked by squads of women wearing business suits, brandishing baseball bats and megaphones. PFM's wife yells in my face behind closed doors. I am rising in the ranks. Join us!

Affirmatory Activity Mind

My community is a-suffering. I'll tell you what. We are given preferential hiring treatment at the point of a gun by the largest government apparatus known in the history of man. That is suffering. We have been handed the "race card" by a naïve and overly accommodating host population that marauded and slaughtered the lone group within its own ranks that expected my community to integrate to the host population. Whenever anything goes wrong, I simply point to the color of my skin. Whenever someone in my community is successful, we point to the color of his skin. This is something to be glorified because our skin color is what defines us, obviously. Yes, we are a-suffering. We murder our host population at eight times the rate they murder us. Our great leaders and rhythmic singers go completely silent on this fact because it would cause a great a-suffering to mention it. Oh, the host group gets us down even further with their *host media*. Do their host media organizations even employ people with our skin color? I'm asking that rhetorically so as to prevent great a-suffering (but we all know the true answer and that's that *yes*, they are forced at the point of a gun to hire people with our skin color). That little voice that spoke in the parenthesis just now was my internalized host population voice. I need to liberate myself or there will be another great a-suffering. Are you enjoying the rhythmic pattern of my speech and tendency to repeat terms often? Good, then give me a lot of your money as you owe it to me because of the great a-suffering. Of course, I am not going to say that explicitly other than this one time because all I need to do is *convey* to you, so that you will be *imbued*, with the sensibilities requisite for losing your identity and knowledge of how my community is 8x murdering your community and nobody in my community is acknowledging it. With this out of the way, we can begin the true process of healing the great a-suffering. This involves…oh, I already said it. Can't say it again. I need to hold these things close to the chest, as a true player does. Gotta "play it to the bone". I can't be foolish like your host community and openly discuss things as a means of expelling malintent.

This is the "hook". I am going to proceed to say a lot of phrases and sentences where the last word ends in "i-n-g". This will produce a hypnotic effect that will allow my community to raise the necessary funds to escape the circumstances we ourselves have been creating. We need to adhere to the host population we've been hating. These times are getting hard, the a-suffering is accelerating. With my preamble and consequent *hook,* I have been contaminating. The youth of the host population have been subjected to massively programmed incapacitating. With my community's charms and low impulse control, these youth have learned to be self-deprecating. They have been infected with a listless, equatorial nihilism that is inebriating. Instead of having a healthy skepticism toward the proposition of a great a-suffering, they have been masturbating. My community does not owe them an apology and to expect us to give one would be moderating. Since the only healthy sense of limits that has ever existed for us has been imposed from without, such a show of contrition would be devastating.

There you have it, another stimulating performance from me, a tremendous thought leader and ancient king. There is a-suffering no more after that brilliant intervention in the shared cultural space between us and the host population. The situation has been profitably massaged and the hosts are assuaged (there I go rhyming again!) You do not like the intricate verbiage of an independent man who is a-suffering? That is because of the color of my skin. In fact, to spite you, I am now going to speak in a more natural manner. Yous a bitch.

In Praise Of Tenderness

Think back and notice how *tender* our old songs were. There was no Leviathan, no "multiculturalism", fiat hadn't yet robbed the working man of his inheritance, and pornography was seen only as blasphemous and vile, if it was even on the radar (and it mostly wasn't). Some somebodies enacted all this. We should log into Minecraft, the video game, and tie their video game avatars to an extremely long row of posts. One of us will walk our video game character over to the many figures tied to posts, put digital cigarettes in their mouths, and then we'll all bust up laughing about how video games are funny. Then our problems will be solved.

Once our problems are solved, we can get back to loving one another again. You can't get to love without going through hell. Sorry, it just doesn't work the "power of positive thinking" way. The *abundance mindset* is just New Age satanism dressed up as a pro-free market, pro-exercise movement. There is no true love without justice. Justice involves moral restitution. Moral restitution requires arrests, trials, and executions of video game cigarette jokes. The can of worms has been opened. I didn't open it. I've spent over a decade trying to close it. If you're my friend, you've been doing your part. Worms taste like shit. I ate one when I was 14 at a bowling alley to make my friends laugh. Worm stomach acid burnt my tongue. I felt like a fucking idiot. It's a nice metaphor for how far away from the tenderness we've gotten.

When wages are robust, the people are ethnically proximal, and the civilization building geniuses are not corrupted by Satan, the tenderness creeps back into the songs. Hymns are had again. Devotionals. The blood of Christ flows. The people kneel.

15

There is rest beyond the river but come on, we know who is contributing to this and who isn't. Not everyone is going to make it. Stop believing Satan. He tells you everyone is going to make it. That is the lie. The truth is that all can save themselves but not all will. Deal with this fact. Prepare for the Rapture. Moral lines are hard and straight. Perfectly straight. And when this Absolute Law is respected, the tenderness comes back.

The voice of Father is speaking to us in the night, reassuring us that the crops will grow, that we will stay warm. That voice is watching over us. The voice is reassuring and encouraging. Soft and gentle and deep as the roots of a redwood. Those massive redwoods, how we miss them. With moral justice, we will bring them back.

Dragged To Hell

There we go again. Diving down into Hell. He and I. I do it willingly. He does it because that's where he is. We visit his demons. They lash us and batter us. The rivers boil with acid. Hallways of mirrors with perverts and goblins visible in the jagged shards of glass lining the groaning, breathing floor. Temptresses dancing, carrying daggers behind their backs. Men in suits, shaking hands and talking loudly. Big-brained atheists cackling like dipshits at the prospect of a Sky Ghost. False tough guys playing sports and getting screwed in the ass by men of other races. Lost children running around in packs, screaming at the top of their lungs in terror because the love oxygen in the atmosphere is running out. They stumble and die, one by one. Comedians with the physiognomy of money-changers standing on stages made of plastic, delivering diatribes about genitalia. Doctors playing for time, hunched over infants in hospitals rife with disease.

Don't worry, it's okay. I am here to acknowledge what you cannot. I am here to say what you will someday find the courage to say. My hope is unshakeable. In time, you will trust me. Then we'll dive even further!

The Empty Pursuit

I see advice-givers telling others to do what they do, "outrun unhappiness". Just compound your secret misery with nootropics! Listen to my magical verbal persuasion once you're nice and high off of the exercise I've barked you through. Smoke cigars with me as we laugh at women not because they're strange and different than us but because we hate them malevolently. All of this, and more, is glossed up with the particular guru's best impression of James Bond 007. It's all so stupid, empty, and boring. It only seems exotic and alluring because there are wealthy people around and because sitting and drinking whiskey with other men is one of the more decent experiences to have in life (compared to sitting at home and watching Netflix). I see these men making their money selling smut, preying on the vanity of any wealthy male that comes in their vicinity, investing in coastal state real estate (where mass migration is skyrocketing real estate prices), charging insecure young men exorbitant prices for basic bitch advice I have given on my platforms a thousand times over, and putting on martial airs, as if they were great leaders when they actually are pursuing a confused embodiment of Nietzschean will-to-power. Patton kneeled to Christ. So did Rommel. I digress.

You can't deny the cleverness of building up an Agent 007 marketing scheme. It's cute. Cute and empty. The fact that this is a profitable venture is more an indictment of the utter soullessness, sexlessness, and uselessness of the therapeutic Leviathan creeping everywhere than it is a valid pursuit, compared to an ideal world. It is, however, a tremendous distraction. While vain men are busy spending enormous amounts of money in order to feel "dangerous", the entire Western world is besieged. If these were private militias being formed in the name of Christ, I wouldn't utter a word of derision. But they're not. And these smut-purveyors and nootropics abusers are sucking up lost souls in order to reinforce the fragmentary nature of our post-feminism, post-Christian West. They are not guiding men back into the family. They are teaching men how to manipulate women instead of teaching them how to disarm women and love them again. They are teaching men to value materialism. They are convincing men it's *cool* to put substances in themselves and talk tough talk. Perhaps, in the upper echelons, these fellows are bringing whores in to sleep with the "attendees". All of this may be "fun!" in the short term but it is a talent siphon out of the true army that needs to form, the one that will set things right in the West. If you want to go off and do your best Baltic/Slavic impresario impression while America burns, you go ahead. You are not going to get any closer to having a higher purpose. You'll simply learn how to be more self-indulgent with your spare time which, to some, feels like a revelation in and of itself. You were more *active*! You got off your lazy butt and got reamed by what you think is an alpha male. Congratulations!

I won't participate in anything like this. My work in this world is too important to place before some psychologically dead, half-breed cosmopolitan simp with mega muscles who makes all the convention rounds. The time is too fleeting to spend pretending to be a baller, an "important" person. The more of an act you put on, the more you get away from what brings you peace and *true growth*. If you want to stay emotionally stunted *acting* like you are very important, you will never become as important as you could be. Instead, you will be self-involved and others who wish to become as self-involved as you are will treat you as important. That is not the same as being important. That is a cult. You are called to sacrifice. We all are. All the glitz and glamour of "being manly" has nothing to do with listening closely and quietly to The Call. I've known about this for a long time. In my 2016 album *Stand And Bleed*, I have a song called "The Call". I meant it then as much as I mean it now. The more bullshit a guru puts in your way, the less he is helping you become. I work with what people bring to me. I do not add anything, insofar as I am aware and as I continue to improve, because I do not have an ego to feed. I do not have an aching desire to become **rich**. My aching desire is to do the right thing. Money may be a byproduct of that but I know, from having spent most of my adult life in poverty despite doing the right thing, that money should never, ever be the goal. Money is nice but it should only ever be the byproduct of a clean conscience.

The Empty Pursuers have to self-justify their coming together. Constantly they harp on and on about how the whole world is set against their coming together, that they're maligned and mischaracterized for doing what comes naturally. Why harp on and on about this? It's because they know they're in a mutual deception together. They know they're building emotional

Ethnic Minority Narcissism

Minorities are encouraged by the Establishment to become self-absorbed and self-involved. Even though America was founded and engineered by Western European men, those men are not allowed explicit representation because of the cultural Marxist lie that people who are the majority in their own country don't *require* explicit representation by sheer virtue of the fact of their percentage share of the population. This is minority ethnic bigotry dressed up in colorful, academic language. Meanwhile, every other population group gets to flout its own perceived achievements to the heavens.

There are Republicans who encourage this type of misbehavior and narcissism. These are radical Marxists who are smart enough not to take on free speech or gun rights directly. They know that if they dilute the host population sufficiently with saccharine ploys for minority representation, they can persist as comfortable managers and social influencers as America nosedives off the demographic cliff. The Boomer generation of whites is particularly sympathetic to this machination. They love the blues guitar. They love how it rips through the fabric of order and inspires other whites to "let loose". They love having a little blues guitar social media influencer in their guitar collections, a little someone they can build up so as to kick the can down the road on their absolute moral failures and total capitulation to the consumerist, fiat, Affirmative Action culture of the 80's, 90's, and aughts.

Anyone attempting to snap American minorities out of their own ethnic narcissism is seen as a *racist*. Funny how the people who profess identitarianism for all but whites are the same ones who throw around the term *racist* in full sincerity. Expect ethnic minorities to not only give a damn about mass legal migration into the West but to make it the absolute centerpiece of their public offerings? You're uncool. You're to be avoided. You're to be shut out of public dialogue. You are to be subtly undermined but never mentioned by name. You are a pariah. Why? Because you are intelligent enough to be hip to the subtle, Marxist nature of the race grift that continues unabated. There is always a war on the most intelligent. The most intelligent, and thereupon those who utilize this intelligence to be aware, are the ones who eventually curtail the shortcuts the less intelligent are taking in order to fuck society into the lesser vision they hold for it. Maybe a minority will pick up this book, process this paragraph, and see the truth in it. After all, these principles are universal. Everyone, from whatever background, benefits from staking all their chips on the mass migration battle at the beating pulse of Western Civilization. Doing so means the death of shortcuts. This is not for the faint of heart and only the most excellent are currently engaged in what actually needs to be done. We will remember who disrespected us in the time to come as these vital arguments continue to make headway into what's left of the culture and public discourse.

You Don't Listen, Do You?

I tried it your way. For years and years, I did. I was a good boy. I sought out your counsel. I put into effect your advice. For a time, it was useful and I was full of gratitude. But then your advice stopped working. You started attending to lower forms, lesser concepts. Somewhere along the line, you lost the thread – at least some of it. Then I waited. I was patient. I figured you'd get *it* back again. But then you made friends with bad people. They gave you bad advice and stroked your ego. You listened to them instead of me and the few others like me. Then I was angry with you. I was angry with you for a while there. You stopped being helpful. In fact, you began to concern yourself with sideshows. It has been annoying. It has been downright cringe, sometimes on a daily basis. Yet, you persist with these bad friends who don't want what you want – ultimately – and who seem to steer you whenever you falter.

I don't need you in order to find my own success. Not all roads run through you - like you often depict. I can do it without you. I am showing others how to do it, too. Your world vision has competitors. I see you actually help sometimes. Not all is lost. That would be to catastrophize, on my part. You're not a *bad* person. You've made questionable decisions and have these agonizingly apparent brain farts that put you in the company of dolts and manipulators. Hey, if that's your prerogative, that's your prerogative. I am still curious to see how it all ends up. You do *just* enough. Maybe that's the point. I don't know. I'm not going to speculate. I can't get that involved anymore. You never listened to me, even in the early years when we had dialogue. I still trust you but it's been years now that I've been arriving at observations and conclusions that you eventually get to or very obviously eventually miss the mark on.

People attack me for having this standpoint. "Get back in line!" they sometimes hiss and spit. The nastiest ones just pretend I don't exist, even though I have helped some of them with some major problems in their thinking or with tremendous pain they were carrying. Funny how that works. If only I were a bit more dramatic, a bit more theatrical, a bit more about the glitz and glamor in my presentation. That's what seals the deal for vain people. But I don't need them. I have never needed your vanity. I have always thought your aesthetic tastes were unbecoming of a grown man. Instead, I have chosen those who cut clean. That's what's necessary. That's all the time we have. My children are going to live in the boogaloo, more so than yours. Best to you and yours, though.

8 AM Chainsaw Landscaping

"Fucking chainsaw landscaping at 8AM on a Saturday. Build the wall."
-Delicious Tacos; October 5th, 2019

The leaf blowers and chainsaws rev up. I'm startled from sleep into a state of confusion and anger. My ancient instincts tell me there's a predator nearby and I should engage in combat. Oh, it's just the Mexican guys my landlord sends every Saturday. I've requested that they come later in the day, probably three times now, but all requests go through the property management company. My landlord is a wealthy Japanese guy who lives in Japan full-time. I shit you not. The basement had bad mold in it from a crack in the foundation and the water table rising too high. My timid basement roommate just lived for weeks with his thin carpets being soaked through. I even see his footprints in the damp carpet.

The shorter, portlier one of the two landscapers is wielding a chainsaw. He's buzzing away on some thick bush. I was up late working last night. Now he's here, ruining my life. The

$2700 a month we pay for this house is split four ways. They reliably raise the rent at least $250 every year on account of Intel, Nike, and a few other companies getting more cheap labor visas every year. Our state has become "business friendly" because it passed corporate tax cuts in order to lure stagnating corporations away from California. The ploy has worked like a charm. Now my formerly-white area has been flooded with ethnics. I can't say anything because of how socially liberal everyone here is. The corporate tax cut is the only remotely "libertarian" thing to come out of this jurisdiction in 25 years. And you have to consider a corporate tax cut within context of other factors, not judge it as a purist would – in and of its own self. A corporate tax cut has simply brought a bunch of people from the Bay Area here and they're all franchising Buffalo Wild Wings and Pier 1 Imports type outfits. Plenty good shopping for the $40k a year Indians and Chinese who live like sardines and swallow up all the real estate. Plenty good eatin' for the sheer flood of Mexicans pouring into the region because wineries and marijuana grow operations are sprouting up left and right. The traffic is abysmal. Everywhere you look, you see the spirit of 8 AM chainsaw landscaping.

I stumble out of bed. All I can afford is a Japanese futon pad. Need to stay mobile, simplistic. There's no settling down here. I see my roommates tending to the coffee. Coffee is for grownups! They're off to their "studies". Basically, they're taking a pounding up the ass from academia so they can become part of a state cartel and make the bigger bucks so they're aren't swamped out like the rest of us who aren't so willing to take on the student loan debt. They secretly hate my guts for being more courageous than they are. I'll learn that lesson in due time. One of them rides out on his bicycle because his parents were poor and dispossessed. The other rides out in a nice Mazda because his parents burrowed-in at the

26

right place and the right time. I hop on my bike. My parents were somewhere in the middle. I have a little pickup I could drive but this area is filled to the brim with cops, eager to write tickets for young men like me. That's the thing about wealth, it attracts over-taxation – resulting in many more "services". Homeless people ride the tram here for free. There's always road construction, at all hours of the day. There are more cops than you can shake a flyswatter at even though the only crime is from the Mexican onslaught and the few whites witless enough to persist in the path of the flood. Money everywhere but nowhere. Lots of clever Californian Gen-Xers and Boomers holed up in their mega houses on tiny lots. This is how it is in every city. But every year, more and more ground is ceded to the 8 AM chainsaw landscaping.

My bike tire is starting to go flat. I'm too stubborn to buy a little pump to reinflate it. I glance one more time at these guys doing the landscaping. With their boots they're SMASHING what's left of the meager sod. They don't give two spits. They're not here as caretakers or groundskeepers. They're here as landscapers. They hit the lawn once a week and move on to another house down the street. They do "the work that whites won't do." We know that isn't true. We know that public schooling utterly fails at inculcating Western values in white students. We know that public schools are a breeding ground for ethnic violence. We know that the young men are blabbed at all day by liberal teachers preoccupied with protecting their benefits and bloated salaries. We know there's no grit being conveyed. Maybe if they watch a movie on the you-know-what, they'll see a little bit of what could be characterized as grit. So much estrangement, so much misery. All the money you could want if you wield the misery. Nothing left for the young people.

27

I veer back toward the house I'm renting and speed by the Mexicans just as they are unloading a zero-turn riding lawnmower from a trailer. This is the $7k model. Not the highest end but let's just say their employer "ain't hurtin'". I point one finger at the taller Mexican and say, "Fuck you!" Instantly, a swarm of police cruisers with their sirens wailing hurl themselves onto my street from the five places you can turn onto it from. These are the aggressive, Charger style cruisers. And a RAM 3500 police cruiser just because our local PD is cash rich. One of the vehicles rams into my front tire, sending me flying into a bush. Twenty police officers, most of them of-color and tattooed, surround me with shotguns and pistols aimed at the center of my private parts. A police helicopter roars overhead, maybe fifty feet above us. None of the police say anything but the moment I start to move, they all shake their heads to dissuade me from moving any further.

The portly Mexican waddles over, revving the chainsaw as he approaches. The police part their circle enough for him to come through. He does a quick, utilitarian job on the bush I'm stuck in. To his credit, he does round the corners a bit more than the other Mexican landscaping outfits in the area do. I'm appreciative. Two female police put me in handcuffs and haul me to the cheap grocery store with the huge overhead fluorescent lights. Outside the store I am put into a pillory, my neck and wrists bound by the wooden frame. This is where I must remain for all time. At first, little Mexican children and extravagant champagne socialists alike festoon me with tubs of room temperature yogurt, tomatoes, and the crueler ones simply spit on me. In time, no one acknowledges me. The police come when I am middle-aged and rotate the stocks so I face the checkout lines instead of the parking lot. This is of great relief to me as I am comforted by the sight of so much vibrant commerce taking place.

Time To Be Rude

"And the Jews' Passover was at hand, and Jesus went up to Jerusalem.

And found in the temple those that sold oxen and sheep and doves, and the changers of money sitting:

And when he had made a scourge of small cords, he drove them all out of the temple, and the sheep, and the oxen; and poured out the changers' money, and overthrew the tables;

And said unto them that sold doves, Take these things hence; make not my Father's house an house of merchandise."

-John 2:13-16; Holy Bible King James Version

Confrontation catalyzes change. The enemy knows this. I wrote about their Alinsky tactics at length in *Rise And Fight.* Sincere immigration patriots and nationalists need a path forward. Some of it will borrow from the enemy's playbook. But we're finding that a lot of it comes out of a knowledge of physiognomy and constitutional psychology. The thoughts you think over time mark your face and define your body. There's a reason why Chuck Schumer looks like Satan. There's a reason why the body language of people, who were successful in the MAGA, Inc era. but have resorted to ankle-biting America First in the new era, appear to us as "compromised" and as grifters. Their spiritual dimension is merchant-like and dishonest. There's a reason why the open socialists and communists appear as if their every movement is controlled by soy products and exposure to housecats.

The thing is: you can only come to know these things if you are spiritually clean yourself. Only then will you come to perceive people at the dimension that is developing. To live spiritually clean, you must be a wholesome person. You must treat your people with love and kindness. Look at the leaders of America First, they're all magnanimous with those who do right. They're severe with those who do wrong. And they're impatient with those who are somewhere in the middle. This attuning power, this barometer for reciprocity can only come out of living Truthfully. Some people call it "authenticity" and granted; it can be authenticity but only if it is living true to the example of Jesus Christ. Any other anchor point is worldly or fabricated. Jesus was the most real person who ever lived. Living by his example is what grants us benevolent power, the power of vision.

With vision, you see clearly what the enemy is doing. America is full of enemies, on all sides. A huge swath of them want you up in the intellect. They want you to trade statistics with them until you're blue in the face. This is not to say that statistics don't have their value, they certainly do, but there is a golden mean. The enemies of America take anything good they can and push it beyond the golden mean so as to tempt good people into their own destruction. The enemies of America cloak themselves in the garb of legitimacy, some of them even professing the Christian faith. Some of them chuckle at the mention of Jesus' name. Some of them act as benevolent non-aggressors, atheist anarcho-capitalists who know enough to know who is good and will pitch in a kind word here and there while maintaining their mainline that "taxation is theft". Of course, we know that is not good enough. We know that men are not defined by how *aware* they are of evil but by how well they *fight* evil. Don't be seduced into a lesser fighting stance because you can't conceive of how race relations would work in the face of multiculturalism and so you have to resort to post-nationalism as a cope. Don't be fooled by these neutral types who made up their minds a long time ago that fiat would wreck society and so the mission is to grey-market the world into statelessness. They don't fight as well as they can and that's what you need to know about them. That's the counterargument.

The time for being rude and confrontational is here. Jesus did it. We have to do it. All in good measure, right? You save your tenderness and love for your family. And in a sense, it is tender and loving to be rude and confrontational with your enemies. When I do these analysis videos where I put the whole vibe of a person under scrutiny, I do it out of love and a hope that they will be saved. That is why I cannot be indicted for cruelty. That's why it doesn't stick whenever some wicked person wanders into the comments section and accuses me of bad faith. Sure, it may be "rude" to liken Charlie Kirk to the backup point guard who fails our small-town team in the clutch, but it is done out of love. And it is the truth. Everyone can have a redemption arc but only if they believe. My rudeness and my confrontation, which happens to be carried out with a sweet and soothing voice not in the slightest pre-conceived or contrived at any point by myself, is done to show these people their own faults to them in a way that does not overwhelm them. That is because I am picking up on things that are already out there, already "in the air". I never close the door on a person who has not already closed the door on themselves. I see open and closed doors in the spiritual quality of the faces of others. Not perfectly but years and years of living morally has my batting rate up there.

You cannot gain this attuning power without suffering and sacrifice. That's why I laugh at the pomposity and indulgent self-importance of Randian acolytes. They sweep the suffering and sacrifice under the rug because of Rand's dumb arguments that were meant to subtly undermine the Catholic faith. She "reasoned" that sacrifice is the surrender of a greater value for a lesser value. That's just stupid framing and lying that a bunch of supposed brainiacs took the bait on. Sacrifice is the death of illusion in order to continue walking the path of meaningful suffering. It is the surrender of lesser value for a greater value. Ayn Rand, you stupid bitch. She set so many people back for so long! What a mess. Anyway, being authentic to Jesus means cutting out the tumors that are killing you – even if it means wielding a rusty, dull blade and doing it under precarious circumstances. There is considerable pain in this. Watch the Randians refuse to give up their massive egos. Many such cases. Doesn't happen to just them. But they and their neocon cousins planted the seeds of what has become a forest of Conservative, Inc. in the Beltway.

Suffer graciously, as best you can. If you endure the underside, you gain the upside. You gain the vision. You gain the joy. You gain the slipstream of meaning running through our world.

Coom Doom

Cooming eradicates your brain's grey matter. Some would refer to this as your midi-chlorians. They'd be right in their assertion! The doom of cooming is unleashed when the hormonal wash of watching another man copulate makes its way across your neural network. You become the Doom Version of yourself. Coomers think to themselves, "What's one more time going to hurt me?" but they don't think to themselves how this thought in and of itself comes from Coom Self. The false personality they've built up begins to take over and think thoughts on the part of the system. It's like coom A.I. All systems become overpowered by the coom doom and the male personality operates in a fashion more akin to a hive, a grey, humming hive of coom people. The queen of the hive is the fantastical, idealized sex partner. Cooming to a woman gives her psychic power in that she becomes a fixture in the personality. This is why heterosexual coomers are so effeminate in their mannerisms and their "humor".

Imagine the self-inflicted doom of a man who has placed at the center of his personality the private, fantastical idealization of what being with his favorite pornstar would be like. He is a man ruled by a woman. We shudder in horror at the idea that Hillary Clinton would have become President and been placed in charge of the armed forces. The coomers almost put her into power! They and the non-whites, let's just say. There's a coomer/non-white coalition out there! One wants doom for their home society by not being able to cope with sexual abuse and the other wants doom for the outgroup out of envy and frustration of the failures of their own societies versus the standard the West posits. Partners in doom. If you think on it some, female porn stars are some of the left's most successful political activists. We ought to round them up and drop them via helicopter into India's busiest slums! Just kidding. Only joking. That was a joke. No, what we should actually instead do is kindly and compassionately explain how the majority of porn performers come from sexually abusive childhoods. When we show just enough compassion, the tattooed childless masses will throw themselves into our arms and instead of impregnating them, we will grieve with them. Then the world will be set right! Some guys just want to kill all of them but I stand against that. Other guys want to outlaw birth control but isn't that against libertarian principles? Libertarian principles govern the world we live in because I say so and anyone who doesn't listen to me just isn't fighting for freedom. Those guys that want to hunt down Jewish porn producers and execute them are dark, twisted, malevolent sociopaths who don't stand for liberty. I disavow.

See, all you have to do is stop watching porn. Then your personality will heal and the profits for the porn industry will dry up. Don't pay attention when someone tells you that the CIA funds the porn industry and that because of banking shenanigans and bailouts that put billions into the coffers of the deep state, the porn industry can run in perpetuity and always snatch up young women (and sometimes children) who were failed by their parents. Don't listen to them! Billions and billions of dollars doesn't make malevolent industries last for generations because all you have to do is just switch off the channel. "Unplugging" from cable television worked out really well for the Gen-X generation, just ask Netflix, Disney+, Hulu, and company.

Wait, I have an idea! We should "unplug" from government, as well. That's totally going to work. We should all start podcasts, call-in shows, and write shitty, pretentious books about the true nature of the free market and how noble idealists can start their own podcasts, call-in shows, and shitty, pretentious books about the nature of the free market. With enough people pretending to like Trump but secretly seething that he is a "statist", and every now and then taking him to task on social media about how he did something that didn't increase freedom in the world, the world will be set free! And remember, we need to be polite emissaries for the message of libertarian freedom. We need to be nice and accommodating to our podcast guests but quietly resent them for not being as anarcho-capitalist as we are. After all, their thinking isn't as rigorous as ours. We have applied the non-aggression principle to every conceivable social ill, business platform, and interpersonal dynamic under the sun. In doing so, we have become the greatest philosophers of all time and we alone stand against the mobs of collectivism and statism! Cooming? That's just a function of the body. Doctors say you're supposed to ejaculate once every two weeks. My anarchist friend who runs a podcast out of American Major Liberal City deliberately avoids discussing the topic of cooming. He's a pretty wise guy. He has like a 150 IQ. Super smart dude. Well-versed on the arguments for freedom. His friends vape. He's not that into fighting against cooming or about naming the ethno-centric group strategies of the different races. There's no need for that when we are all in agreement that universal principles can be observed by anyone, regardless of color, creed, or coom. We don't have to address coomers and non-whites specifically because Hayek and Mises would have looked down upon that. Plus, also, my anarchist Jew buddy in Liberal City would quietly ostracize me and drip droplets of *total and absolute truth* into the ears of our mutuals, being the tremendous philosopher that he is. Stout anarcho-capitalists like him are not standing in the way of freedom. You started to think that, huh? You are showing me signs that you had a disturbed childhood. There is no argument against people talking blandly about how big government is bad using rehashed Stefan Molyneux talking points (that he learned from his predecessors) while Rome burns. There is no argument against posting "questions" we already know the answer to but aren't willing to answer publicly because we'd rather put on the show of feigning curiosity as a manipulative way of steering people toward libertarian ideals. There is so much time left in the West to point out how the left is hurting itself. Whole states are turning blue but don't you worry, one more tweet about central banking or about how Singapore is super frickin' cool simply has no counter-argument. Coom brain doesn't play into this!

A libertarian tolerance of people engaging in sex work, while making vain overtures of compassion so as to not completely piss off the Christians in our audience, has no crossover with coom brain. Coom brain would never drive a person to feminine abstraction in the face of brutal hordes of child rapists, rioters, and looters. Grandstanding with anarcho-capitalism as one's backing ethical framework for the West's final hours is a completely viable, effective, and universal approach to dealing with the fires that aren't being put out. Also, we should expend a lot of breath on what is going on in other nations. That is an important way of humanizing out-groups and pacifying, therapeutically, the discontentment in the people most screwed over by the ongoing legal dispossession of whites in the United States and Canada. Jews had a wedding in a bomb shelter while under duress from Palestinian rocket fire? Totally a humanizing moment. It's super-duper important to highlight so as to maintain a contrived "middle stance" on what bigots are calling the *Jewish Question*. The last

36

thing we want is to upset anyone and besides, you could characterize anarcho-capitalism as a Jewish ideology if you really want to get in the weeds on what political movements were ethnocentric in nature. And my friend, you don't want to do that because I am far more experienced than you in intellectual matters and no one has ever offered me a piece of corrective feedback that has even in the slightest altered any fundamentals of my worldview.

I don't want to hear about how early Jewish anarcho-capitalist thinkers made entirely no effort whatsoever to acculturate their concepts with the host white population's folkish, Christian sensibilities and that anarcho-capitalism's conveyors, for the entirety of its duration as an ethical framework, have been purely logical, and largely economic in their disposition toward potential converts. Hong Kongese are proximal to anarcho-capitalists and that is a great mystery to me. I will pose it as a confused question on Twitter because that's good, nootropic style copywriting (though I could just as easily trace Hong Kong's roots to Cantonese merchant origins closely watched over by a British banking class that held a fever grip on the institutions). I frankly don't have to listen to you about this because you're being verbally aggressive and I'd rather spend my time posting about how central banking is bad and how the Armenian genocide has not been acknowledged for a really long time. Coom doom and anarcho-capitalism are not mutually beneficial, corroding forces on the psychic mechanisms of moral courage. Porn is aesthetically negative and preys upon childhood sexual abuse but I would never break the NAP to put a stop to it!

PowerPoint slideshow featuring images of people of tropical "heritage" dressed in the garb of scientists and lawyers. They are shaking hands with one another. Everyone is happy and successful. Then the images slowly turn to violence and chaos as more and more white men make their way into the images. The kids are incited to terror and they flee for the exits. Their middle-aged female teacher calls after them about how they're right to exercise their *multiple intelligences* by going out to the schoolyard where their limber bodies can exercise.

I turn my attention to the city canal, a stone's throw away. Up until the last five years, nobody fished from the canal because it was common knowledge that there are heavy metals in the canal from our city's industrial years in the 1970's. I see men of a different complexion than mine fishing from the canal. They are using roasted weenies and bulk sale lunchmeat as their bait. One of them catches a turtle. He immediately smashes the turtle against the concrete sidewalk, over and over. The turtle is bleeding and dead. His friends hoot and holler in delight. I begin to feel angry but then the secret agent steps in, blocking my view. He says to me, "Steve, you race-hating jerk. You need to keep it positive. If you can't keep it positive, at least keep it boring so that your viewership eventually plateaus and people at-large consider you a non-starter." I nod at him. He steps away.

I look out onto the open field where some good old-fashioned American families are delighting in the play and tussle of their apartment-dwelling chihuahua dogs. These dogs are not "like family", they *are* family. They're running so wild and free. They're chasing each other as if they hadn't a care in the world. Their spectacled, Patagonia-wearing owners are beaming with pride. I can see civil union bands on their fingers. They're all happy. Out of nowhere come some better, improved Americans with pit bulls off their leashes. Oh, the slaughter! I'm seeing chihuahua guts flying in the air. Their owners are calling the police. They have nervous looks on their faces. This is definitely not good, they must be thinking. One of them is so stressed that she has set her coffee down on the ground in order to call her chihuahua's name out in concern. The chihuahua, with a pit bull latched to its neck, utters a blood-gurgling cry, "Bark, bark!" I see in the background some neckbearded 115 IQ white guys laughing at the bloody scene. They high five each other before turning their attention back to the pornography they're watching on a shared laptop. The secret agent steps back in to block my view. He says to me, "Steve, you're so crass. Your writing is so cynical and myopic. You're not successful. You never will be because I'm not going to let you have a seat at the table. If you want a seat at the table with the other adults, you must learn to be less offensive. You are making light of people's suffering. That's not okay. Now you are on a watchlist. Good luck getting a job as a graphic designer or in middle-management." He points his finger and laughs at me. He forms his hand into a gun and makes a shooting sound. I hand him my credit card and he hands me a job with his agency. Now I can pay my bills and not sleep on a park bench anymore!

I Will Not Eat The Bugs

The man from Manhattan is making eyes at me again. He knows I'm *different*. Just how, he's not sure. He knows I'm too intelligent to be working in this place, serving him his wild-caught fancy food wrap while Sam Cooke plays over the intercom. He moved here after a brief dalliance with San Francisco. He just adores the public transit, the makeover the whole downtown is getting, and that he can walk around freely with his fanciful body language without suffering scrutiny.

Look at that, he gave me his phone number. What a thing. He's seen something he likes and he wants to ritualistically spoil it behind closed doors. I won't go, of course. There's a whole ethos here that sucks young men into sexual soirees. The homosexuals have an intense liberal culture. You pick up on it in the magazines on the stands. You see older men with younger men. There's an especial lot of older white or Jewish men with young, non-white men. Some of them get married. Most don't, though. You can see they get off on the spectacle they make of themselves. Their culture requires they remain "sophisticated" about it. This involves eating wild-caught fancy food wraps. This involves shopping at the corporation I'm working for. The outward appearance is to be wholesome. The true nature of this establishment is to provide a kind of catwalk for deviants to be seen by one another. This is as true in mountainous Colorado as it is here, American Liberal City. This lecher man is one of the stars of the show. After all, he's from the Big Top. He's seduced more clients than you can count. For the more masculine ones, he has a small dachshund he parades around. The dachshund serves the same function a single mom employs when she puts her children in her Tinder profile.

What this man wearing high end, tasteful designer clothing and $1000 spectacles doesn't know about me is that I know the way out of his madness. He's not the first Manhattanite of his kind that I have come across. I know most of the sophisticates, whether by study from afar or by the intellectual meanderings of what most could consider my "career". His type is not unknown to me. I know the scene. I know what people of his age, early to mid-60's, did in their heyday. I know how they marched on Washington. I know all of it except what it feels like to, you know, copulate the way they do. I don't bear the mark and I never will. But to know who is declaring themselves your adversaries, sometimes it is useful to get a closer look. Who are the architects behind my legal and spiritual dispossession? They've written books? They've had whole documentaries made about them? I can speedread and watch films on double or even triple speed? Wow, there's a lot I can learn about these colonists from Hell. Outer space. Bizarre mountain regions from far away. People think I'm speaking in double entendres but I'm not. I'm talking about space lesbians here.

I'm going to give him my full legal name, knowing he's going to Google me. A man of his intelligence doesn't get to his age doing the things he's done without having a knack for some Internet research. Look at that. He's avoiding me now. He doesn't like what I've posted about my knowledge of the things he's into. He doesn't like what I have to say about the family. My art runs contrary to his. I'm not going to come up to his 12th story apartment and "have tea" with him. Nor am I going to ride the elevator up to take care of his dog when he's back in NYC. His snares lie empty. I can almost see him curse under his breath. I would have been a hell of a catch for him. The crown jewel of his beyond this. This is as far as the intrigue goes. Actually, let me tell you about the impeachment scandal. Or the Ukraine problem. Those are probably even more primary to the situation at hand. You want to get into conspiracies? Have you heard of wage gap? It's actually a myth.

The Subverters

They're out in full force. Some of them are so strong, so well-entrenched that you can't even name them, even in private circles. I'm not going to name them here. They're powerful! The time for naming them will eventually come. They know it. I know it. Each party hopes the other will change and make the necessary concessions. Maybe we'll never see that day. We have bigger fish to fry, in the meantime. Obvious turdheads who are on full display, making a terrible mess of everything. There are people who throw gays off of buildings! There are jihadists operating within America's borders. These are people specifically orienting their entire intellectual machinations to be operating fully against the *actual* populist uprising that America needs to have in order to save itself, obviously. Nobody is more dangerous to America right now than Alexandra Ocasio-Cortez. She's a socialist. Or how about Elizabeth Warren? She's a Native American. That's funny. It's also a meme. Yeah, she's a big threat.

Let's deal with the obvious baddies before we deal with the more entrenched and sophisticated baddies. That's a winning strategy. We have a lot of time to be doing that. We should be scoring zingers on CNN. We should be showing people how super intelligent we are by fact-checking left wing journalists who flub some esoteric detail of the impeachment scandal. We need to win over the /r/The_Donald audience with one more palatable retweet of a *Daily Wire* puff piece about how this one black guy who smokes weed got invited to The White House. That's important stuff. We need middle-aged female supporters of Trump in 2016 to feel at ease with us. We should not be challenging them to save the economic and civic futures of their children. We should be assuaging their anxieties by focusing intensely on our branding. Did you know I'm a brand specialist? Yeah, I organized that one community clean-up. The President retweeted me when I talked about a minority group decimating the "competition" in what is purported publicly to be a free market (but that we privately know is a market bazaar nestled in the shadow of the Leviathan). Like Paul Ryan said, and I know it's a little unpopular to bring him up these days but what he said was substantive, "In a free market, nobody's success comes at the expense of anyone else – there's simply just self-interested parties doing voluntary exchanges with each other." I like that talking point because it makes me forget about how there hasn't been a free market in the United States since central banking was instituted by a small group of dynastic cool dudes.

Another thing I like to do with my massive platform is constantly wage psyop battles for the benefit of a foreign nation. I do this through choice, tasteful retweets of op-ed pieces and foreign outlet reports that paint a pretty picture of this foreign nation (that may or may not get me some payola through indirect channels that I would rather die than disclose). I also expend a lot of flatteries onto anyone, irrespective of their political orientation, for what I perceive as competence. This looks good to the middle-aged 2016 Trump supporting women who I sometimes hit up for focus group data. You could say I'm a bit of a chameleon but trust me, deep down my motivations are sincere. If you think I'm kicking the good guys in the balls every now and then out of pure sadistic lust, you're incorrect. These nut-kicks are actually well thought out, precision point strikes meant to put people back into line (my line…don't tell anyone I said that). What the mainstream media doesn't want you to know is that I have a deep, analytical super-mastery of Correctness Thinking. I am on such another level than CNN and the FakeNews media. My analysis of the situation with Ukraine is Machiavellian. Come see the tweet they don't want you to see. You see, the actual enemies of America are like a *House of Cards* and I've been training my whole life to defeat them in hyper-intellectual combat. Correctness Thinking is like kung-fu but for smart people. Best you leave this to the experts, kiddo. I'm the grownup here. I'm more mature than you. I praise people for competence, even if it's in the service of evil, and that's *nuanced*. You can learn a *few* things about the art of Correctness Thinking if you go and read this super long red herring book that this one super brainy, non-political person wrote.

Oh, look, the hour is late. I'm just getting started! Now I'm promoting that semi-Indian white British kid who looks like he's permanently going through pre-puberty while making overly baroque songs that give people the distinct sense he's being groomed for wealthy black homosexuals who have fled to the Middle East to escape English-speaking scrutiny. I'm all about peak performance. America is sliding into chaos? That's CNN's fault! Thanks for the memories. Now I'm promoting that African-born British rapper who speaks things into existence and is totally hilarious. If he needed some branding advice, I would probably give it to him but pro-bono because my career is mature enough that I'm doing things altruistically now. Intellectual kung-fu masters like me like to keep up appearances with the super successful. Who knows what wrong-thinker I will blow out of the water next!

.

Managed Decline

A big fish kissed the ring, today. He knows it. We all know it. A lot of people are letting him know. He's earned the ire that is coming his way. He lied and kissed the ring in one fell swoop. Now his output has finally crystalized into the bland, rehashed sideshow I have been warning people about for a few years. Nobody can say I didn't try to help when it mattered. There's something going on that we don't know about. That's about the only way to explain how strong people buckle and bend the knee in such a rotten manner. Are these people receiving credible death threats from intelligence agencies, foreign or domestic? Looks that way. Are some of the people that are prominent in the Trumpian movement actually federal agents who received extensive intelligence training in the years before Trump's run? Looks that way. I don't know for sure, so I won't speak with certainty. But it looks that way. Our strongest guys either kiss the ring and humiliate themselves or they get murdered. No, our *strongest* aren't the ones who spiral out and lose their focus. I'm talking about the guys who cut clean. The 140 IQ and higher guys who have the Faustian spirit. The only way a guy gives up the Faustian spirit is if well-organized death squads pay him a visit, especially if he has children. We know from the pizzagate stuff (that everyone prominent has quietly pushed to the side in favor of impeachment and Ukraine crap) that the people who run the world are absolutely Satanic in their treatment of children. Drawing and quartering them. Other unspeakable stuff. A Faustian bends only to that threat. He does not bend because his thinking eventually goes awry. No way. The truth is WAY too clear. The truth is far too huge a landing zone for a man's proverbial helicopter to utterly miss. Yet, it happens. Or the guy is murdered.

The Faustian starts the process of crumbling and eventual ring-kissing when he lets into his social circle those who deal in dark arts. These are people who use mind-breaking drugs, are unwilling to publicly swear off foreign fealty, mysteriously have friends in high places, have tremendous sums of cash to dole out, are particularly litigious, are surrounded by rumors of sexual escapades, or even are so brazen as to just *tease* the possibility of occultic rituals taking place at the elite events they go to. The Faustian gives up his fundamental Western nature when he goes outside of himself for "advantages". There is no advantage outside of himself, only folly. Don't be fooled. The "Western Tradition" is not Abrahamic. It is Jesus. There is no way outside of Jesus. Jesus is the life spring of self-knowledge. There are a million and one tricks the devil plays but there is only one way to Jesus. Why do you think I rail against Rand and her Randians? Why do you think I warn about the pitfalls of libertarianism and anarcho-capitalism? You must stay with Jesus. Jesus lived. He died for our sins. He is ascended into Heaven and seated at the right hand of the Father. Look at the men who turned their back on Him. Look at the men who came to know Him but then acted with arrogance and defaulted to some peckerhead stuff about "not being able to explain the phenomena of consciousness". Look at the men who spend all their time trying to define Him instead of being open vessels for his Will. There's so much arrogance in the West. There are so many dumb people shouting on the Internet with their cowardly opinions. And then there are people even dumber than they with outright evil opinions.

The thin, fine line is to convey as much truth as possible without provoking the hysteria of the Persecutors. We know what they're about. We know who they prefer, who they spare, who they prop up. We have seen their revolution over and over again. Some men just give up on dancing the thin, fine line. They go back to their "hits" and give up the burning quest. Some are threatened with murder and they bow out. Some are threatened and persist still, until they are murdered by a shot to the stomach in some public place by some random person without a past. Some just never had *it* and they spiral out. Some men do everything in their power and then quietly help the younger, up and coming men who have even more vigor. I like those old types. Not many of them left in the world now. You could probably count them on two hands, maybe even just one.

Nebraska

I am up late driving where the pines grow wild and tall. I'm bleeding from my chest, right where the heart is. I don't know if I'm going to die or not. I'm not too concerned. I feel light. I remember my childhood. I remember my innocence. I remember the owls calling in the night. There was more wildlife then. Now there's lights everywhere. I don't notice them so much. I feel the blood running down my white shirt onto my jeans and pooling in my lap. I feel the leather bench seat. My hand is on the shifter. I'm driving away from the lights. I'm driving away from the people. But I'm bleeding out. I don't know how far I'm going to get. There is a voice in the night calling me, like the owls when I was a boy. Back then I was little. I was scared. My daddy would take me out to look at the stars. He'd take me out for the full moons. There's no moon tonight. There's just the voice calling me away and the blood running out of me. They're never going to catch me. They couldn't, even if they had the speed. But they don't have the speed. They only got a bullet through. But I don't mind much now. I'm going there now. I'm going to that voice. I drive fast. Now it's silent and still. I look up through the trees.

Jokes About The Big H

"Bro stop saying six million didnt die it isnt funny. Bro stop. One mustn't joke abt things like 9/11, big H, jeffrey epstein, the las vegas shooting— that's no good." -Nick Fuentes; Nov. 21ˢᵗ, 2019

Acting like jokes in this vein are at the expense of historical victims is insincere. We all know that government has been shoving down our throats particular narratives, statistics, and forensic details that haven't held up under scrutiny.

Elie Wiesel came to my middle school leadership class (for kids who tested at the upper end of things) and spun yarns that didn't match up w/ his written work on the Holocaust. He told story after story about kids dying in gruesome ways while the teachers put pressure on the kids to feel sad and that this was the most tragic thing that ever happened. By the end of it, all the kids were overwhelmed and crying. Mission accomplished.

Elie Wiesel, it turns out, has been a prominent hoaxer and lent his name to all manner of discredited stories about the Holocaust. Oh, but certain people "dislike" jokes about the Holocaust? There's a whole industry pumped through the public schooling system to traumatize non-Jewish children w/ horror stories about the Holocaust. Make a joke that gives some of these victims an outside perspective that could help them to disentangle the trauma they went through? That's grounds for finger-wagging, shaming, and performative disavowals.

What a fucking joke.

Fuck anyone who says you can't make jokes about these kinds of events. The government is destroying people's lives with this shit.

Elie Wiesel literally asked if there were any kids of German descent in the classroom.

Imagine the shame programmed into a kid who's part German after hearing a well-practiced, grandiose monologue about Jewish kids getting blown to bits and the ground "bubbling with blood" by a NOBEL PRIZE winning authority who's constantly getting talked up by the teachers - and this "wise" old man asks who in the classroom is part-German...

The unending jokes at the expense of the part-German kid after your high school social studies class watches Schindler's List (even though you watched it the previous school year). "Watch out! He's going to become Hitler!" and other stupid shit like this. And don't even start on the kind of bullying non-white kids will put the part-German kid through on account of these movies.

And most of the Jewish kids leave public school to go to private high schools, academies, and other institutions specifically for Jewish kids to succeed. They don't have to give two flying fucks about what the non-Jewish kids go through (but notice how this doesn't run both ways). Jewish kids aren't forced to endure the Holodomor Unit or the Armenian Genocide Unit when they're in public schools. They don't have to hear Kurdish speakers telling them how Saddam gassed women and children, nor the gruesome details of people suffocating on their own spit.

So, how about we have a bit of empathy and compassion? When you inculcate millions of students with what amounts to horror porn, you are participating in a psychological Holoc*ust of the American mind.

How about we don't reflexively freak out when someone has the balls to shed a bit of light on this with a joke or two?

You need not get sucked into some forensic back and forth with some person who has a personal grudge against you for the jokes you make. The exact facts of history will never be settled. Don't play their game. Point out what's happening in the public schools. Point out how the children are being traumatized for something they had no part in. Point out the lack of reciprocity and the special emphasis the curriculum places on children suffering. Point out the horror porn.

Trained Simps

I have watched various platformers "train" their audience on how to interact with them. Everyone does it a bit differently. There are some guys who want HIGH ENERGY for the sake of high energy. They need people to get high with. Some guys are weaselly shitheads who invite a bunch of drama into their lives. I immediately stop paying attention to them when I pick up on this. I don't need that. Some guys are *absolute sharks* who will pump anyone they can for any performative advantage. These are the guys who you feed "tips" to.

A couple of things in particular that I have appreciated have been:

-Nick Fuentes pointing out people being cringe and stupid in their Superchats (unafraid of social conflict in dealing with Dunning-Kruger dummies but also deftly sweeping them to the side)

-platformers who cultivate masculine respect for a man's time

I want for the people who reach out to me to be of use to me *first* before they expect me to do an analysis video, comment on some e-drama, or give a bit of advice. I'll tell you now how you can be of use to me: leave a positive review for one of my books (including this one!) on Amazon/Audible/Goodreads, send me money (via Paypal, a monthly subscription on Patreon or through my website, or Bitcoin), buy one of my books, or sign up for one of my video series through Gumroad. There, with that out of the way, what's up? I'll tell you: my time is limited. Keep it to three paragraphs or less. Give me a tip on a good e-drama to analyze. Let me know how my work has impacted you. Give me the good news. Ask me about setting up a consultation session. If you're an artist, send me fan art or something that's beautiful – if it's good, I will promote your work! Put me in touch with platformers who are *larger* than me that could increase my exposure (since I'm awesome and about as on-the-money as a person can get). Add value to my life and I'll be grateful.

The title is "Trained Simps" because I can't stand platformers who use their influence to flatter their own egos. You see this in their comment sections. They respond to those who flatter them. I don't want your flattery. I don't want you to "patch me up" if I'm down. I can deal with what this life will throw at me. Thanks, but no thanks for the sympathy. I'm not Jordan Peterson.

I'm a self-contained person. Nor do you need to throw *high energy* my way. What are you, crazy? Nor am I an *absolute shark*. I'm not looking to screw someone over to get ahead. The truth is good enough for me. I don't need 20 paragraph emails about some minor foible you perceive a contemporary of mine committed. Start your own platform if you're that hard up to express something! Be courageous in your own life. Support and lift up those around you. I send money *all the time* to good people on our side. And I'm not overflowing with money. I do it because I want it revisited upon me. And I don't talk about this publicly because I don't want a spectacle made of it. Even now, behind this paywall of having to have bought this book to get ahold of this message, I highlight this only to illustrate the point of building others up instead of pining for their attention. If I'm a pass-first point guard who's taking your team deep into the playoffs, then you know I know what to do with the ball. Funny to think of it that way cause over my adulthood that's how my role developed in pick-up basketball despite being trained for years and years to play in the post as a kid. That's my natural personality. I pass first. Treat me the same way. Respect the rules of the game, so to speak. Don't kiss the ball and then speak to it for fifteen paragraphs before passing it to me! What are you, stupid? You're disrupting the flow of the game.

I have a tremendous capacity for insight and analysis. And I'm not swayed by temptation. I've done my time in the desert. The few guys who get here don't get here until their 40's or 50's. I've been here a while. I'm helping others to get here in a much more expedient manner. My time will end up becoming extremely valuable (the value of it now would blow 18-year-old Steve Franssen's mind). I will never forget Donald Trump's example of preferring to spend time with the construction workers on job sites (over their bosses) and how he pulls people from the crowd. I will never forget Bolsonaro walking on the beach with his fellow Brazilians despite being stabbed out in public less than two years earlier. When I am near my zenith, I will not forget those who helped me out along the way. Nor will I forget those who insulted me, wasted my time, spread rumors about me, or ignored me. I don't want simps. I don't want followers. I just want to do things the right way and see others do the right thing. Our time together is limited, so let's make the absolute best of it!

Suggestibility

There is a woman walking by, here on this city street. She's dressed well, as if she works in a law office somewhere. Taking a second here to process. Okay, got it. She's a whore. She hangs out at clubs, takes MDMA, and has sex with random men. You can see the alcohol consumption in the quality of her skin collagen. Collagen doesn't come back, despite what the scientists and celebrities tell you. There's honest skin and then there's whatever the hell Halle Berry and Sandra Bullock are on. You can see she's a cardio addict by the lack of healthy skin fat over her sternum. She's talking on the phone now. Yeah, definitely a liberal. She's got a coffee in her hand. It's 5:15 PM. Thirsty Thursday!

I've decided I'm going to stalk her. I'm laughing to myself now the same way a dastardly fiend from the silent movie era would. Don't worry, I'm not going to tie her to the train tracks. To achieve that, I would need to batter her over the head while she wasn't looking. I'm not a violent guy. I just like people watching and learning what I can. But I do like stalking women. That makes me laugh. I like the secret power I feel over them. Since they're never technically in danger, the courts can't put restraining orders on me. Some rich women have managed it but I don't stalk them anymore. I try to only stalk firmly middle class or lower middle-class women.

I've been waiting outside of her apartment building for a few hours now. I have a 30-stitch gash over my left eye because a black guy decided to try and kill me for telling him he was being rude outside a pizza parlor. He hurled a street sign at me, point blank range. I was in the city news for a night. Waiting here, patiently. She doesn't have a street-facing window. I don't know when she'll – oh there she is. She's dressed like a total whore. Time to follow her!

She's going on a date? That was unexpected. He's a Middle Eastern looking fellow. They're hopping on the subway. I'm two cars away from them. They know each other already. They're speaking as if they were familiars. I choose to be homeless, you know? They're getting off now. I'm tailing them like an expert. There they are behind a restaurant in an alley. She's giving him a blowjob. He's smoking a joint. This is interesting to me. I put my hand in my pocket and resist the urge to stimulate my member slightly. I try not to look at his face. I get nervously excited as they turn directly toward me but calm down when I realize it's just the direction they've chosen to walk. I'm an unassuming, homeless man sitting on the concrete. I get over my chub. I'm keeping my distance.

I can see they've gone into a different restaurant and this time there's a window view for me. This place is swanky! They're meeting with wealthy people. The Middle Eastern guy is some mid-level dude compared to them. She's an armpiece. I just had a funny idea. I'm going to do it. Haha, I just ran up to the window and stuck my ass cheeks against it. Glancing over my shoulder as I ran away, I could see they were perturbed. That was my moment of madness. Let's see how they respond. I'm hiding behind a tree some distance away at the edge of a park. An SUV pulls up and takes the wealthy men away. My lady is still with her Middle Eastern man. They're snorting coke in plain view. Nobody cares. I care. I dated her once. That's my confession. We went on one date. She turned me down. I waited two days and then texted her to see if we could get a follow-up date. She said the chemistry wasn't there. I asked her what could have been better for her. She didn't reply to that. Now I follow her everywhere. I know what she does. It's hard for me to track her when she gets into cars but since I know where she lives, that's just where I default back to. I've wanted to learn *why* she rejected me. So far, all I can come up with is that she's a suggestible whore and I wasn't mean enough to her. She'd be better off with me. Both you and I know it.

The Mean Man

There lives a mean man in a treehouse. He kills birds in the forest with blow darts and then eats them. He does not like people who have different levels of melanin in their skin. Not only that but he denounces them to the rare people he meets on the forest trails around his treehouse. This upsets people. The authorities won't do anything about him because they can't find him. He is deeply elusive. Sometimes he is spotted scrounging mushrooms by the river bank. Helicopters with infrared vision have been sent after him but he's too clever for them. He has many burrows he dives into to evade their detection. Then, when people least suspect it, he pops out of the burrows to yell racist things.

The authorities have sent trained Vietnamese burrow crawlers after him. These are the sons and daughters of Vietcong. They are world class rabbit catchers, under normal circumstances, but their skills have taken on new meaning in the face of the mean man's menace. The sad thing is that these Vietnamese burrow crawlers aren't very hardy. He lives in a permafrost zone. The Vietnamese crawlers often freeze to death. There have been a number of their corpses found in various stages of cannibalization. Ooh, he is one mean bugger.

Sometimes he leaves notes on their bare chests, jabbed into the flesh with sharp twigs. One of his most recent notes read:

Dear Townsfolk,

Your fears and suspicions are confirmed. I am indeed a mean man. I single-handedly destroyed the United States of America. Want to know how I did it? I made mean jokes that people of good taste did not approve of. Worse than that, I am also guilty of thinking impure thoughts. My thoughts and my words, that are deeply racist in nature, have brought your civilization to its knees. But no one can capture me because I am too elusive.

You see, I was raised by racist bigots like myself. They did awful, terrible things to me like give me enough food to eat or kept me away from the pedophile government. This abnormal, you could say extreme, upbringing granted me the superpowers that are on full display now.

Be careful and watch over your children, especially in the night. I have decided I am going to circumvent your home security systems, kill your shepherd dogs with poison, and then come tell stories to your children after I crack open their bedroom windows. I will whisper unspeakable, cruel things that any reasonable person would find offensive. Then I will return to my treehouse and laugh as you vainly comb the territory for my whereabouts. There is nothing you can do to stop me!

Signed,

The Mean Man

We have undertaken the strictest countermeasures to thwart his efforts. From our sacred minarets, recently constructed by valiant Moroccan men, we blast out beautiful prayers from holy texts. This is designed to drown out the voice of the mean man. We have sent droves of bush-beaters into the wilds to flush out all the birds. Last week we killed 45 birds. There are few birds left to kill but still, we rest uneasy. There's an urban legend going around that if we mate our sons and daughters to the Squid People, The Mean Man will no longer have a hold on their minds. In actuality, this hasn't worked. We've simply been left with a bunch of squid/human abominations that we feel uncomfortable around but raise as our own.

Nothing yet works against The Mean Man. He's so very mean and we clench our fists at him, wherever he may be. "You bastard!" I cry into the night but my wife comes and brings me back inside from the back porch. I sob and sob at the edge of the bed and she consoles me by rubbing her hand on my shoulder. When will he stop tormenting our northern town? When will the central government send Murder Robots to root him out like it has to the other Mean Men. He may be the last of his kind. That means that all of the power of the other Mean Men has been concentrated into him. He's like a mega juggernaut. Only Murder Robots have ever beaten juggernauts.

Mask Off

I enjoy the lyrical content and overall sonic atmosphere of the rapper Future's song *Mask Off*. I have long sought to understand cultures different than my own, not out of feelings of supplication but out of a sincere desire to relate – or at the very least to be better guarded against sectarian aggression. I was first turned on to this song when I took an Uber in Salt Lake City to the airport and an African person who barely spoke English was the driver. They had this song playing on the stereo loudly, without regard to the rider's experience. I have had similar experiences from all non-Western drivers. Something about this song was different than the other big songs at that time. I went on a tour of all the major hip-hop songs of the previous six months. I watched the *Mask Off* music video and then understood why the song was relevant to me.

The music video depicts Future riding around in a foreign luxury car while feminist e-whore Amber Rose straddles him, blowing smoke into his mouth. There is a convenience store robbery. There are men brandishing weapons at the camera while plumes of fire burst everywhere. The scene is one of total pandemonium. One comes to notice that there are Hispanic gangsters and that they are allied with the black gangsters. They all dance a shuffle toward the end of the video with one of Future's crew leading them. Many of them are wearing large masks with oversized teeth. This is a depiction of the eventual riots that will grip the major metropolitan centers of the United States when a third world saturation point has been achieved. There's one lyric in particular that stands out to me, "We gang, they gang. But they are not the same." This is the last verse lyric of the entire song, which consists of extensive drug use, flying around the country, drug houses, and violence. This lyric demonstrates perfectly the in-group, out-group awareness of ghetto culture. Just before writing this essay, I was watching a video of a black woman screaming incoherently to a rebellious youth sitting in an NYPD vehicle before opening the door so he could make his escape – all the while still handcuffed. Among the ghetto culturists, a term which does not encapsulate all black people in the United States, there is an extremely high time preference that is marked by high impulsivity, proclivity for violence, and an inability to formulate higher order enterprises that exclude the baseline "smash and grab" commerce of large swaths of the third world. *Mask Off* is perhaps the most explicit acknowledgement that ghetto culturists have an in-group identity and are eager, not just willing, to do violence upon the out-group.

These are purveyors of economic and social ruin. You can see their world vision come to life in their music videos. Another prominent ghetto culturist is the talented vocalist and untalented dancer The Weeknd. His veneer is more sophisticated than

Future's, probably on account of less drug use, but you still see the cult of economic catastrophe in his music videos. This Michael Jacksonesque performer routinely breaks 1 billion YouTube views for his videos. These are probably phony numbers, but never underestimate the global appeal of hip-hop and its predominating ghetto culture persuasion. I am most certainly aware of Kanye West's efforts to bring all of the best purveyors of hip-hop out of the ghetto they have been mired in and back into the service of the Lord. I celebrate those efforts and am merely making commentary on the still-growing identitarian efforts of ghetto culturists to bring the United States to its permanent ruin.

I compare this "world vision" to that of semi-obscure Celtic folk rock band Iona. Their song *Treasure* was made into a music video that currently sits at 6,860 views on YouTube. The video features the band, led by talented female singer Joanne Hogg, dressed in artful, traditional clothing and playing their instruments around a Scottish castle. They are smiling, the directing is similar to the early 90's Spin Doctors style, candles are lit, there are intricate instrumental solos, and Joanne is singing out:

> *If a son asks his father on earth*
> *For fish or for bread*
> *Who among you would give him*
> *A snake or a stone*
> *How much more does the Father above*
> *Have a heart full of love*
> *For the children that He calls His own*

This vision for the world has a Christian ethic and speaks of that which is treasured. Were I to have David Geffen's $8.5 billion net worth overnight, which vision for the world would I promote? Both acts, Future and Iona, are talented in their own way but it is undeniable that one act wants Western Civilization to buckle under the excesses of the street drug cartels and the other wants people to have fun with their families on tastefully manicured lawns beneath a sunny sky. One act has under 7k views and the other routinely gets over a billion. Which world vision is coming to fruition?

If you look into it, you'll find that Iona's band members ended up becoming idiot multiculturalists. Joanne helps third world invaders to Europe gain access to aid materials and other such nonsense…all while she happily walks her expensive horse along the northern Irish coast. Don't think I idealize these people. For a window of time, Iona made some wholesome music.

A word on, "Steve, make your own music video and let it compete in the free market of ideas". First of all, fuck you. With that out of the way, let me resume the pleasantries. There is no free market because central banking has been instituted in the United States for over a century. Since there is no free market, there is no "free market of ideas". The federal, state, county, and municipal governments already dictate considerable control of what is acceptable discourse. This makes its way into the culture. Beyond that, the hell spawn of government – corporations – has been busy amassing extreme bureaucratic leverage over the culture on the backs of utterly disastrous internationalist trade deals that have robbed the American worker of *everything*. I should just make my own Twitter, eh? Oh, but Twitter higher-ups are demi-gods empowered with the ability to de-person others. These are people who get massive kickbacks from importing docile coolies who will work for slave wages. Time for me to compete! If only I had access to millions of dollars for a single music video that expresses how the American worker has been gouged for almost three generations now. Too bad the American worker has no money left. Too bad the only people who have money anymore are managerial elite who are either outright socialists or pretend on the surface to be Republicans. You literally have to live near a Federal Reserve bank or a $10 billion plus net worth corporation to have even semi-decent healthcare and money earning prospects.

Suddenly I am in the same VR chatroom as the person who told me to "compete in the marketplace of ideas". I am an oversized Garfield The Cat with a Pikachu tail. He has a plain looking avatar that reminds me of something Mark Zuckerberg would craft for himself if he had friends around to play Dungeons And Dragons with him when he was a teenager. I dash over to Plain Man and start zapping him with my Pikachu tail. He is screaming out in agony as the electricity makes his skin cook, forming boils on his skin. He screams at me for breaking the digital non-aggression principle and that he will take this up with the local corporate council. He begins to walk away to go through the portal that leads to the Elton John Fans lounge when I grab him from behind with my Garfield claws. I throw him up in the air. He screams like a stuck pig as he comes down and lands in my digital jaws. My sharpened cat teeth gouge massive holes in his plain body. I spit him out in front of a shrine dedicated to an anime princess. He lays broken and dying. I walk up some digital steps and when I am at the top, I yell, "Eat your heart out, centrist!"

Fight Feminism!

Did you know that feminism is bad? Yeah, it's the most bad. That's why I dedicate a significant chunk of my posts on social media to how feminism is bad. Feminism tore apart the traditional family. Feminism made women unhappy. I care about women's happiness because I am a noble man. Statistics show that feminism is bad. Many different statistics:

-50%

-72%

-21%

These are important statistics. I am important because I am sharing them. Did you know if a woman is a whore, she is unhappy? Your mind is pretty blown right now. Did you know that if a father isn't around, the kids have less impulse control? I know these facts and many other facts. Since I know these facts, I am prepared to be a parent figure to you – irrespective of your emotional maturity compared to mine. Feminism is bad. Let me dress you so you look like Ernest Hemingway. You look handsome! I'm proud of you. Proud of you like your father never was. I am your father. I, am your father. Fathering you, now.

Did you get the statistics? Good, you're going to need them to *hold frame* when a toxic feminist comes into your midst and tries to isolate you from your fellow men. BLAM! Hit em' with statistics. They won't know what hit them because they're not statistical. They're egotistical. And I am alchemistical. I know the secrets of Western Man's personality. I have read *The Prince, Art of War*, and *48 Laws of Power*. I read them while artfully smoking a pipe and making other men laugh. We looked like a vignette from a *Time* magazine from the 1950's. Band of brothers. Ah, I remember that day well.

Ernest Hemingway was there, you know. Yes, he was telling us statistics about how feminism has made women unhappy. We gathered around. There was little breathing room because our shoulder muscles are quite developed. He told us the secrets of manhood. We were in a barbershop run by Jack Gristle, the toughest son of a bitch that ever dealt in statistics. Ernest slammed a beer mug on the table and roared, "Women, we love you! We want to see you be successful. You have the power to remove us from the gene pool. Put down your ideological weapons, my sweet damsels." We hooted and applauded his valiant efforts. What a man! Our ruckus dislodged from the wall a wooden plaque that read, "Don't use the f-word and never talk about race publicly." I dove down and caught it just before it hit the floor. Everyone gave me a swell pat on the back, including Ernest Hemingway. Jack Gristle smiled at me from his standing desk. He was eating a plant-based diet to help him recover more quickly from soft tissue owies he got from playing tennis with his 51-year-old wife. He says she's the funniest person he has ever known and since he has unending credibility with me, I consider her the funniest person I have ever known. He wants her to be happy. We all do.

My sons came into Jack Gristle's barbershop. Their names are Buck, Jack, and Bo. They're all tall compared to the other kids (some feminist told me that they're average height and I'm below average height and so therefore I'm over-excited about their prospects but I slit his throat with statistics). My sons began to wrestle and talk about how they wanted to be God when they grew up. I smiled like a loving patriarch. Oh, boys. My band of brothers laughed heartily and patted me on my nicely developed shoulder. Jack offered me some of his plant-based diet but I just said to him, "Brother, there's more than enough for all of us. Abundance, my king." He pounded fists with me. Us eight men or so pulled out our pocket knives and began whittling various things like walking sticks, Pinewood Derby cars, and compasses. Ernest Hemingway smoked a cigar and drank a mojito. He described to us how he loves the way the alcohol pours over the ice cubes. I was super helpful to him and told him my favorite variation of the mojito: the dirty mojito. That's when you whisper anti-feminism statistics into the shot glass as you're pouring the drink and then you give the shot glass a little pat on the ass for good luck. Learned that one from a petroleum engineer who was known for his deep concern for the happiness of women.

I remember that day like it was yesterday. For some strange reason that annoyed me, all of the buildings outside were on fire and race rioters were dragging police to their deaths by the dozen. Bankers in super drones were sweeping down from the sky to scoop up white children and put them into what they referred to as "collections" in their basements. I'll tell you what, though, feminists were crying liberal tears because of the fun we were having. Never let anyone get between you and your fellowship of noble philosopher kings. And don't ever let a feminist tell you how to prepare a drink!

Hitting The Big Time

Businessmen, philosophers, polemicists, and coach-athletes have gathered outside of my door here in Montana. There's a tremendous hubbub. Their voices are buzzing with excitement. I stand up from my undersized leather recliner I'm too stubborn to sell because I'll be selling it at a loss and I haven't owned it that long. Alright, alright, I mutter to myself as I amble to my porch where everyone is gathered. I open the door and am immediately assailed by a cacophony of everyone's best YouTube voice. They're all giving me a gritty monologue along the lines of, "Dear Steven, you are my friend and longtime listener. I value your critical opinion. In case you haven't noticed, the liberals are *at it again*!" I hear music playing in the background. I can't tell if it's circus music or metal-rap.

Their monologues continue, "We have formed a coalition of the best and brightest contrarians, libertarians, conservatives, freedom fighters, black revolutionaries, Chinese Leadership Summit attendees, anarcho-capitalist economists, and embattled moguls who have said sympathetic things to us in the press. We have all come together, Steven, and we agree that we have found the ultimate leader of our movement. He has proven himself, time and again, in the face of tremendous scrutiny."

I am picking up pieces of this monologue because everyone is speaking it at the same time with slightly different pacing or voicing. They finish by saying, "You, Steven, are now completely and totally convinced of the worthiness of this individual because we are persuasive, argumentative, factual, and analytical. This person, our great leader, is the rhetorical, political, and philosophical nuclear bomb the civilized world once feared Stalin would rain down upon the West – but the Democrats are the real racists! So, without further ado, let us present to you the greatest leader our movement has ever known."

I wait for a moment while the stragglers finish with the extra particulars that distinguish them as entertaining and thus worthy of much higher YouTube subcounts than the majority of those present. When they are done, they begin to part the way by stepping backwards to reveal the great leader that has come to show me the path to ultimate victory.

I strain to see and then suddenly a dwarf is before me. He is three feet tall. Pressing up against his dress shirt I can see he has areolas the size of pepperoni slices. One of his arms is visibly shorter than the other. His brow is abnormally thick, like a caveman. I can clearly hear circus music playing now. He opens his mouth to speak and a wretched, scratchy voice comes out, "Steven, our greatest ally is in mortal danger. Will you bend the knee as others have? We know you have noticed even the most subtle bending of the knee on the part of people you have trusted for years. Notice, they are all here now." The dwarf pauses to sneeze into a tissue. He clears his throat but the scratchy voice returns, "You are literally powerless to stop us." Walking into view are my two favorite YouTubers, guys who have been putting out choice content on the daily for years now. They each have a pistol pressed up to the temple of my faithful dog, Moose. "Just join us, Steve. You prefer 'Steve', don't you? You have resisted overtures and undertures from our most sophisticated operatives for too long. We're sorry it had to be this way. But, we want you to choose *willingly* to come with us."

I stare at all of my favorite platformers. I look at each of them in the face. Their faces are all eager and positive. The circus music makes the mood feel bright. I know they're all sincerely counting on me. They've helped me so much over the years. They've given me incisive political and philosophical commentary for so long. They've taught me principles about optics and other cool stuff. They've sometimes made me almost laugh. Gosh, they are truly counting on me this time.

Then I look at my faithful dog. I see something much different in his eyes. I see sadness there. I make up my mind in that moment about what I must do.

I sprint at the dwarf and punt him with the full strength of my leg, sending him flying ten feet into the air. Metal-rap music EXPLODES all around me. My dog escapes his captors. We stand back-to-back and fight off all of my favorite platformers until eventually they club us to death.

Subtle Assertiveness

Third Worlders have a difficult time distinguishing between assertiveness and aggression. At best, a few of them get it. But most don't. The more enlightened ones respond to assertiveness with passive aggression. These are the ones who consider themselves *Western*, even though they're not. Others in that camp include the ones that respond with *extra* assertiveness, as if it were some kind of high stakes poker game. These people are so boring and middling. They're tiresome.

Native Westerners understand the art of assertiveness. They've been stewing in it for generations upon generations. They know how to respond to someone who is finely tuned in to the needs of the situation at hand. They get the West's notions of leadership and the distribution of responsibility necessary to "survive winter." They have an intrinsic understanding of when to defer, when the *little guy* should step up, and when the "big dogs" are taking care of things. Third Worlders don't give two spits about this subtlety. They show up to the Austrian ballroom dance and spit on the floor, shake their hips, and yell loudly when they're politely asked to leave.

The West is a beautiful, artful dance – much the same way. But many of its natives have been brainwashed out of their natural instincts, inundated with the hordes, and worked to death by corporations and governments that put on a benevolent smile. Duels should be a thing again. You see it rising up a bit with celebrity boxing matches. Nobody is saying might is right but the West needs a release valve for the tensions that are building up. Dueling with pistols favors reaction time, a huge marker for IQ. Americans should be allowed to "duel" with foreign drug gangs. There's no need for the FBI, DHS, CIA, and others to fight Islamic terrorism within America's borders. Just allow the Italian and Jewish-Russian mobs to deal with it. Rather than allow for a bit of friction in the short term and peace in the long term, the government is busy sending SWAT teams after Xbox thieves and babysitting migrant children at the border. Let the patriots round up border-crossers. Friction up front so extreme bloodshed in the long run is prevented. This won't be allowed. And so, someone charismatic, intelligent, and calculating enough will come to the fore and do something about it. So be it. A revolution of that nature would reestablish the West's cozy foundation that allowed for all manner of higher order assertiveness to play out. People treated each other differently when mutual combat was legally assured. People treated each other differently before security cameras and cell phones allowed for every misstep to be seen and then attended to by a militarized police force. People actually tolerated thievery, robbery, assault, and vandalism a lot less before the days of super surveillance and the Third World braying of, "Call da police! ¡Llama la policía!" People were *forced* to reason out their problems because there was no globo-homo Leviathan eager and at the ready to arbitrate all disputes between private parties in favor of state power. Everyone loses, the government wins. "Sir, yes sir. With my life I will uphold gay marriage, sir!"

Competence used to be able to assert itself. "Get the fuck out of my way!" the scientist madman funded by tycoons used to be able to say. The philosopher ahead of his time used to be able to get his books published and then have a small apartment for himself from which he would take long walks. Everything is inverted now. The greediest shitheads all flock to the American coasts and grab what they can, posturing as if they were civilization builders in the process. "Look at me! I own a 3.6-million-dollar home right on the Bay. I was an early investor in Vitamin Water/Fleshlight/Uber." Nothing ever gets stripped back. Nobody makes money stripping back the long, bloody march of government supremacy. Nobody gets rich undoing the interstate highway system. Instead, a few San Francisco dickheads get mega rich slathering Uber over the top of the pre-existing system. Nobody gets rich busting kids out of public schools. Well, a few do but it's done under the auspices of school shootings in order to funnel kids to child traffickers. Mostly, people get rich scoring big Department of Education contracts to put operating systems into the schools. Or people get rich distributing to the schools low nutrient, processed foods grown on poorly managed land cultivated by immigrant sweat labor. The Forbes richest men in the world made their money by filling in some exploitable niche created by Roosevelt's New Deal or Johnson's Great Society or Kennedy's Hart Cellar. Or the other top rich men (we're not including the Red Shield Banking Clan here) made their money by building up big portfolios including what these niche men "carved out". Would computers even exist in their current form if Edison hadn't ruthlessly fucked over Tesla out of spite for Tesla's superior talents? Should the automobile industry even exist or would its iteration of the last 70 years have been completely leap-frogged over by something superior if WWII hadn't happened?

Modern man is increasingly encased in the dazzling entrapments of billionaires who dandy and bandy about as if they were truly important. They fly to this state and that, going to meetings and investing money tastefully. More and more shitty housing developments pop up everywhere. More and more Africans get jobs as orderlies in American hospitals. Our gadgets go faster. Our food incorporates more and more insect "protein". Yet, somehow, the contemporary construction of banks is the only *quality* construction across thousands of American towns and cities. The bank is literally the only decent building erected in the past 50 years. Middle American men have no access to the quality of building materials that existed in the 1800's. Therefore, there are no true risks being taken. Everything is starting to look uniform because corporations run by billionaires dictate the appearance of everything. And they get all their kickbacks from the state. Instead of working with marble, the common American construction worker (we used to call them "builders" and "craftsmen" but what they do anymore hardly qualifies as anything more than paint-by-numbers) has to satisfy himself with putting dyes and epoxies in concrete. And this kind of "artisanry" fetches a huge price tag because millionaire Boomers and coastal businessmen like the novelty but also the cost effectiveness of finished concrete. What a sick joke. Everything is degrading. Nobody is getting wealthy doing *the right thing*. Hardly anybody wealthy is even trying to tilt things back into the *right* direction.

Every Man A King, Huey Long used to say. The Middle American deserves so much more than he is getting. He is getting so much less than he used to get. His chances at joining the wealthy are slimmer than ever. Middle Americans used to sometimes join the wealthy and, in the process, do a bunch of creative and out of the ordinary things that inspired others. All across America there used to be *attractions*. The largest ball of yarn in the world was just the tip of the Iceberg. Disneyland used to be just a cool theme park before it became a whole culture, rife with Satanists and militant socialists. There used to be World's Fairs. High school students used to be into rocketry! Now high school students ward off physical beatings from Tyrone, brow-beatings from middle-aged cat ladies, and constant surveillance from school officers placed in nearly every school post-9/11. Property taxes keep going up, services keep degrading, the soil and timber reserves keep getting gouged, porn keeps getting proliferated to new venues, and millionaires and billionaires in the wake of the Leviathan prance around like they're big stars and important people.

It's sick. The whole fucking thing is sick. Who will give the American Worker the true spiritual succor that was once his birthright? Who will populate the CDC with micro spy drones that will bring to light their malevolence? Who will tear down all the

BLM buildings scattered across America's great expanses? Who will *actually* Build The Wall? Who will let the Latino and black gangs simply fight it out until one capitulates once that Wall is actually built? Who will take away Walmart's performative advantages so that the Ma and Pa stores can come back? Who will use the Navy to bar all trans-Pacific freight to and from China so that small American manufacturers can begin to find their feet again? China is literally building ethnicity specific pathogens to kill off white people and we're supposed to be dazzled that Elon Musk built a terror truck for the boogaloo? What utter tripe. What a gutter America is in. What complete lack of humility and honesty on the part of its civic leaders, for so long. You millionaires and billionaires have been *warned* for generations now by true populists that what you're enacting needs to be peeled back. You don't listen, do you? The rails have been split by the *Establishment*. We're barreling toward total annihilation and you want to frame me as some fringe, lunatic fascist because I want to put us back on track?

Despite what abundance-signalers and Randians would have you believe, doing the right thing is not always doing the profitable thing. America has $23 trillion in national debt, $120 trillion in unfunded liabilities, and the taxpayer's share of this debt is $788,000. Persisting aggressively in the bizarro business environment that exists under these conditions may be the lot of sociopaths and grifters but it is not what will set civilization back on course. People who actually give a damn are *sacrificing*. Most of these people are Middle Americans, and yes, there are a few millionaires among them, maybe a billionaire or two. Children are being enslaved through debt and the only people doing anything about it are the ones with the stones to speak out against the *rampant* pillaging that is taking place **and** not participating in it by getting in the way of true populists, such as the folks I am constantly promoting on social media and in my books. You either fund Buchanan or you're in the way. The same could be said about Trump in 2015/2016. Other, natural populists will rise up. To those of you making money off America, Inc. I say, "Pay your penance." And the more you pay, the more of a moral conscience you buy for your children and their future. All is not lost because you're taking a paycheck as a school teacher or scoring DoD contracts for your tech company, but you better be tithing a large portion of your paycheck to a cause greater than yourself. And there is no better cause than *America First*, which is the will of God.

D'Angelo's *Voodoo*

One of the absolute best albums to have ever been created was D'Angelo's *Voodoo*, which turns 20 years old here in just a bit. D'Angelo was dissatisfied with the direction of R&B music and decided to create something that would honor the past masters. He brought the musical focus back onto the groove and onto virtuosity. In these respects, and others, *Voodoo* is a masterpiece.

There's a word, *traditional*, that gets floated around a lot these days. *Voodoo* is an approximation of that word in the sense that it carried a torch from the past but reached new heights in the present. The same animating ethos that pushes me to read the past masters, consume every angle of their writings, and press my abilities to new heights is the ethos of *Voodoo*. There's a *bareness* in the sound of *Voodoo* that has always made sense to me. For each song, D'Angelo stripped away everything but the absolute essentials and then honed and honed until the groove was complete. The vocal harmonies layer perfectly. The drums are perfectly off-center in a manner much ballyhooed by music reviewers. The claps are perfectly mic'd. The song structure always carries you back into the groove. You're never left hanging. *Voodoo* is a great work of love. The album was crafted before substance abuse and other excesses got the best of D'Angelo's innocence. He put something out during a window of time that may never be replicated because *Voodoo* was not self-conscious, as all other purported "masterpieces" have been since. The album is as precise a musical delight as a vocalist or instrumentalist could hope for. And echoes of its glory were brought back to life when D'Angelo famously performed 'Untitled' and 'Sugah Daddy' at the 2012 BET Awards. He left the absolute finest black artists of the day completely stunned and *shook*. In the audience, you see complete and total concentration on the performance from Jamie Foxx, one of the bigger "music heads" of the black community (famous for accurately portraying Ray Charles in an Oscar-winning biopic). You see Kanye West completely transfixed, in contrast to inauthentic Beyoncé – who is standing right beside him and *showing* others how she's enjoying the music. Rarely does peak musical virtuosity come into contact with the spirit of traditionalism, of stringent adherence to the rules and guiding intent of a form. *Voodoo* accomplished this.

The bounds and form of R&B music are well known to those who honor its canon. I have learned much from the principles at work in *Voodoo* and from D'Angelo's career, in general. The institution of R&B was a fertile ground from which D'Angelo's brilliance has sprung.

The tie-in here is that there exists a rising force in dissident, what could be termed "right wing", politics that builds upon the forms already perceived by previous masters. As silly as it sounds, we're cultivating the ground from which a "Smaller Government D'Angelo" will spring from. It sounds silly! But bear with me: Perhaps the person is already alive and well, putting down the roots that will allow them to grow bigger and stronger than has yet been seen. How do we hack at the size of the state, bring back white racial consciousness (which indisputably *did* exist prior to the World Wars), and create a healthy environment for family and traditional Christian values… in the face of stultifying congressional bodies, unending Third World hordes, and a crony capitalist lobby with infinite billions in their coffers? It's going to take a "D'Angelo" or two, right? It's going to take someone with such a tremendous grasp of the realities at hand that their *artistry* will rip a hole in the social fabric, whereupon all proceeding efforts will have to readjust.

Of course, all the "anti-racists" (who exist simply to enforce the current banking order), will freak out and screech about Adolf Hitler at this point. Tells you about their guilty consciences. They can't conceive that just how D'Angelo helped millions with his music, so would a dissident politician. They immediately assume this will be a punitive figure (because of their guilty consciences). They can't perceive the fun that looks to be just around the corner. The dude that successfully wrangles the Leviathan, and the tools *do* exist – we're just working to see who will wield them all, will be a hell of a virtuoso. Our job is to build up that man within ourselves and to build up the men who have the stones to actually attempt the "full wrangle". And the parasites leeching off of Middle America will scream and screech as if austerity measures are being put into place (even though it's just government spending being cut). They will harangue Middle America about how this man is blah-blah-blah. But if we march onward and have the belief that there can be pure artistry in this life, that someone can rise to the top and carry millions over the finish line out of sheer mastery – then we deserve that man when he comes.

The Benevolent Chicken Farmer

The Flynn Effect is "the substantial and long-sustained increase in both fluid and crystallized intelligence test scores that were measured in many parts of the world over the 20th century." When you dig into intelligence research, you figure out all sorts of wild facts – like Victorian era people were 15 IQ points smarter than people of today. You can conceptualize that by going to a local grocery store in Nebraska somewhere and imagining that every person in the store is at least as smart as a modern-day app developer or college professor. The West had *ditch diggers* who were as smart as high school teachers. You learn fun facts like these and a whole nother cavalcade of facts that make you see the globe in a much different light. We'll save that for another time.

A common refrain in the intelligence research community is, "The Flynn Effect is reversing and we *don't know* why!" These people make a huge, theatrical show about how they're utterly baffled as to why people are getting stupider. Since they don't have direct correlation, they often don't care to take an educated guess as to *why*. I'll do that now and save you the pearl-clutching.

The Flynn Effect is reversing probably because of:
-mass migration to the West from low IQ populations
-mega sized governments put downward selective pressures on the environment
-smart people have been bamboozled into not having children

Let's start with the first, and I'll only cover it briefly as I have just given it a treatment in my book *Dead West Walking*. People from the Third World are much dumber than people from the West. Mind you, IQ scores from East Asia and from…Israel, are higher than native Westerners. Nobody is a "supreemacist" here. These are just the facts. When you import 70 million dumber people (some of them are indeed marvelously smart) and then force the native population to intermix with them by every avenue possible, you get a dysfunctional society wherein the dumb, loud people rule the roost. Chicken farmers have known this for eons. Same goes for every livestock farmer under the sun. The dumb, aggressive breeds dominate once they have numerical superiority. And until then they cause all manner of grief and complications (relative to the gentler, smarter breeds). Keep the aggressive chickens in their own chicken tractor and they will do *OK*. Force them to mix with gentle chickens and suddenly all their territorialism and low impulse control is activated. This isn't rocket science. Set down your racism pitchforks: Jews and Asians have been documented as having higher IQ's than whites. But not everything boils down to IQ. But a lot does!

Clown World is a meme because there's an obvious psychosis to the sound the social fabric makes as it is rented by the hands of mass organizations. What isn't a meme, because it isn't as sexy or catchy, is the concept of DMV World. I don't hear anyone positing it in these terms. I do hear *The Great Slowdown* thrown out there. At the DMV you have to wait in line, often for hours, until your number is called. The DMV doesn't care if you're short on time. The DMV has no incentive to change. The DMV has remained trapped in time since its inception, as are all government institutions. These institutions only degenerate as they gobble up more and more market share. These institutions favor the dim-witted, the handicapped, and the deviant because those are the only kinds of people who are willing to tolerate such a grinding work environment. Dim-witted people need easy, apparent rules of operation. The handicapped are at a performative disadvantage and require accommodation everywhere they go. The deviant live unruly private lives that are best sustained by a steady, predictable paycheck with outdated responsibilities and a large measure of difficulty in being fired. As a result, these types are far more incentivized to procreate than they were in a leaner, more personal employment situation that forced them to be moral, excellent, and constantly revising in order to be disposed to the needs of the clientele. Since the American dollar is printed willy-nilly by whatever group of ~65-year-old sociopaths are at the helm of the particular generation and since the "economy" is somewhere around 55% dominated by the "public sector", we all live in the shadow of super massive government. Government picks the winners and losers. Government always picks the simps, dullards, vampires, perverts, and psychos as the winners. Doesn't mean that every now and then a populist will emerge who is made of sterner stuff and "cleans house". But generally, this is the exception to the rule. The gene pool from which a populist can emerge has continually degraded as more psychos sign away the opportunities once available to decent people.

The other thing is that, in order to import a more docile workforce, the psychos at the helm have convinced people to have less children. In particular, they have focused on the more intelligent. The more intelligent also happen to be the more empathetic and so when they are sold stories of global decimation via overpopulation or that the environment is being raped to death by pollution, they drop like flies. Of course, the anti-natal propagandists neglected to mention that it is actually in the Third World where most of the global "cancer tumors" of overpopulation and pollution are spreading. One of the more prominent Planned Parenthood advocates to have lived, Mary Lou Tanton (wife of immigration patriot John Tanton) actually spent all of her Golden Generation years convincing white, rural Michigan farmer women to not procreate. Now look at Michigan. Great job, Mary Lou! Maybe you should have cast your gaze a bit further! Rather than publish their pamphlets on global warming and overpopulation in Hindi or Somali, the Club of Rome guys out of Switzerland targeted America and the Western European nations. Some of the highest recorded IQ's have been in Norway. Where should global depopulation advocates base one of their field offices? Norway, of course! That has been the logic. It's so flagrantly downright stupid that you start to wonder if it has all been on purpose…

How do we make the West smarter again? Most of the IQ researchers or enthusiasts start acting like Goofy when this question is put to them. They fidget and fumble and then whoopsie-daisy, they fell down the stairs! There are a few of them out there with balls, I'll hand it to them. You have to halt and reverse these trends, duh. You don't need to seed the Third World with iodine and go around shouting to everyone how breastfeeding increases neural density. You don't need to wish upon a star with

CRISPR gene editing (engineered smart babies). You don't need to guffaw, hem and haw as if the Flynn Effect's reversal is some great mystery to you (that's a bitch move). You need to start confronting people with the facts of the West's decline. Tell them the truth about *legal* mass migration. Tell them the truth about the Leviathan. Tell them the truth about how China and India are far and away the world's worst polluters. And encourage intelligent people to have as many children as they can. Help these people return to God. Be a benevolent chicken farmer. Some people would tell you to cut the coaxial cords of 5G towers but I am not going to say that! That violates property rights!

Ugly People Who Don't Listen

The worst thing you can be is ugly and not listen when better ideas come your way. At least when you're *actually* pretty, people want to fornicate you. Ugly people who don't listen, don't respond positively to better ideas, surround themselves with anyone they can that's *actually* pretty. It's a smokescreen. That's 99% of marketing: surround yourself with glamor while you rob the society of whatever it is that you feel is a deficit in yourself. Elite child rapists are terrified of their own mortality and utter lack of creativity. Grifters don't sincerely believe in God. Political operatives are secretly afraid that they're witless and autistic. Philosophers who focus on regality and solemnity secretly worry that they're making asses out of themselves. Comedians who make penis jokes secretly worry that they've destroyed any chance they have at true happiness. Bankers secretly worry they're destroying the whole world and so they double down. Actors worry they're phonies. Musicians worry they're utterly incapable of expressing their madness through words. Not all people of these vocations are imposters but the ones who have to sell their words other than simply speak them are most certainly imposters. And the easiest smokescreen for an imposter is sexy people.

Sexiness throws all sorts of wrenches into a man's ability to think clearly. Men who are vain and stupid think they can harness this and so they fashion for themselves impressive coats of muscle armor. All they've done is themselves become the wizard they were worried they were susceptible to. Men who are vain and scared a woman will take over their lives do nothing more than simply "up the stakes." Women hurt me! Now I'm going to make sure they never hurt me by making sure I feel good about myself by having a bunch of muscles that will throw people off the scent of my insecurities. Dumb. So fucking dumb. But guys like these make buttloads of money because everyone's been hurt by a woman. That's the original betrayal. Your mother screws up somewhere along the way. The person that birthed you into this world and sustained you at their breast will always and inevitably fail you in some measure at some point. Rather than deal with this by thinking back on it in a self-knowledgeable way, men invent all these stupid but convincing postures in order to trick themselves into thinking they're not vulnerable to women. But they are! They then have to keep up the charade when they get a woman. You see them getting their pictures taken at arbitrary red-carpet events and taking vain, expensive selfie pictures at this swimming pool and that swimming pool. Men do all sorts of stupid things because they're bewitched by women. And wealthy, manipulative men either harness this sexy witchcraft onto their fellow man (as certain successful tribes do) or they are *simps* who suckle at the nipple of marketing. You, dear reader, don't have to be either. But you have to be willing to have a bit of self-knowledge.

Historically, men built coats of muscle armor in order to *kill their enemies.* Now men do it in the same ethos of "women dressing up for each other" and enemies overrun the land. Unless you're going to use your muscles for what they were naturally intended to do, shut the fuck up and develop your language skills. We're getting pulverized into a billion pieces and you're coping by worrying about other men's bodies. That's gay! And here's a reality check for all the vain men out there hypnotized by the witchcraft of marketing: pulling the trigger on a rifle doesn't require a 300 lb. bench press. Gamers get such a bad rap from "manly men" because video games are a "waste of time". The "manly men" won't be so tough and posturing when mech suits, drones, and other Boston Dynamics style machines come to the fore. All that preening will be for nothing when some Zoomer or Generation Alpha kid, who regularly batted 8:1 Call Of Duty kill-to-death ratios, is put in command of one of these machines. The world is dominated by "cyber security", at present. Do you think eating game meat, doing your best Joe Rogan impression, and body shaming slender gamers for having "squirt gun arms" is going to matter one iota when the Japanese-Chinese Mech War is in full swing?

The truth is that the young man who is busy developing his language skills and his reaction time is the beautiful man who listens. He knows what will be required of him in the future. He knows that if he has to do some version of the old 20th century nation-state war, Basic Training in six weeks will get him up to speed so he can die the old-fashioned way. And it's not going to play out like that. The open, curious, and Christ-like man of today knows that Jesus wasn't *lifting heavy* with Simon and John. They know that he was verbally adept, quick with the reaction times, calculating, and ultimately, did whatever was necessary to keep his Covenant…including die on a cross. Come on, bro, you think that simping after women by "raising your sexual market value" is the secret to life? That's retarded. Jesus didn't simp. Jesus didn't worry if a man had big muscles. Jesus wasn't gay. Jesus wasn't seduced by marketing. He didn't go around practicing marketing on people. He just did what was required, he did what was necessary. Nothing more, nothing less. And he was beautiful.

Don't be like these ugly numbskulls who dress themselves fancy and surround themselves with the trappings of marketing. They aren't "business people". They're professional liars! They're exquisitely good at what they do but all you have to do to make them shrivel like the spiritual imps they are, is to call them faggots. That's all it boils down to. But don't underestimate the tremendous SPACE they inhabit right now. Why do you think I'm dedicating several essays over several books to them? They'll steer humanity right over the brink and right now, they've got at least some of a grip on the steering wheel. The seducers are everywhere. The seduction of Trump is in the air. He is not fully Christlike. Don't be fooled. He was banging whores at the Playboy Mansion with the best of them. His daughter is a national embarrassment. The amount of surgery she's had in order to look the way she does is *marketing*. He is not a Savior. He did his good part to keep the Leviathan at bay but he did not pierce the Leviathan through the heart. And now the ugly underside of his personality has become the common American culture, at least among those who profess virtue in today's day and age. For as much as Trump helped in 2015/2016, he has also kept some sorely needed things from happening. This is the ethos of the modern incarnation of the grifter. And these dudes BLOT OUT the information space. Many roads funnel back to them because they reflect back to everyone the spiritual maturity of the nation. No more! We don't have time for their spergery. We need to put it to these cockheads because they're the ones who will simp the West into oblivion. Stop doing their dance by reacting to the eternal Mama. Start acting like a man!

Panicky Men

Few things I can stand less than panicky men. Few guys you can count on less than panicky men. What's the worst thing that's going to happen to you? You die? Your family is raped and tortured to death in front of your eyes and then you're tortured to death? You can be horrified by that. Did the last quarter of your dick get sliced off by a doctor acting under orders from Satan? Do you remember how excruciatingly terrifying and painful that was? If you haven't remembered, maybe you need to. Maybe you need to sit in a quiet room with the lights turned down, watch a medical video of a circumcision, and then *empathize* with the forever-agony of that little baby boy. You'll probably be overcome with extreme emotions. Go ahead and feel them. Let them course through you. Let them change your identity. Now stop acting like a circumcised simp. Stop panicking. You're dragging the rest of us down. You're allowing for more circumcision to take place in the world. Don't think for a moment the circumcisers don't have *killers* at their disposal. Don't think for a second they wouldn't hesitate in fucking slitting your throat for opposing them. Most of the time, they don't even disguise what they're doing. They just do it out in the open. Our guys are fucking dying out there. You don't get to panic anymore. You reexperienced your circumcision. Grow up. You're not the only one.

The circumcisers want us pissing our pants when the heat gets turned up. They *idealize* the guy who shits his britches, clinging to his rifle and groveling while the rest of his squad is blown to bits. They want serfs. They want simps. Why do you think they're cutting millions of cocks the way they are? Cutting the end off of your dick leaves you with such all-pervading mental and neurological scarring that you will never get back what was your promise. They know this shit. They've been doing it since ancient times. You don't need to fight a brutal war. Convince your enemy of the Promise of circumcision (which is a blessing only if your True Lord is Satan) then flood their society with porn. Then the men lose their fighting spirit. They lose their ability to differentiate. They lose their protective sleeve in all things. Don't let them get away with this crime. Protect your guys. Become the sleeve that protects the innocent. Don't become the butchery they hexed you with. There's torture and genocide porn everywhere. That's deliberate. It combines with the loss of the foreskin. The massively programmed Western mind shatters in the face of that forensic evil. Look how the Nazis are depicted. They are always imbued with the extreme, scientific butchery of Mengele. That's the reality of today. Why do you think sex change operations are broadcast on network television? This happens because no one pushes back on our guys dropping like flies. *Saw*, *Hostel*, and *The Purge* happen all the time. The doctors have free license to do so. This seeps its way into the broader culture. Now you can't even say a word to a bearded drag queen without being accused of being a mental abuser. And our so-called "dissident leaders" don't raise their voices up. Weaklings. Putrid weaklings. And what do you think anal sex with circumcised penises does to the deep human psyche. What prison do we live in where this is openly tolerated and accepted by the "dissident leaders"? What a far cry from sanity! No wonder there are some who are just totally opposed to the industrial revolution.

Our leaders piss their pants because the circumcisers have killers. And the only way to put fear into their killers is to promise to chop off their testicles in the process of torturing them to death. What a sick doctrine everything has come to operate under. And the *panicky men,* what do they do? They piss their pants because they can't handle working full-time. They piss their pants because *women are mean.* They clutch their rifle and sob because America is *expensive to live in.* They let Third Worlders boss them around. Enough! Go relive your circumcision. Process the experience. Now help your brothers out. They're dying out there. You're lazing about the barracks, flexing your muscles in the mirror or practicing how you appear to others. What faggotry. Patton was right to slap the shit out of those two men. And the entire media establishment painted him as a tyrant. Maybe he should have slapped the shit out of some more people. Maybe that kind of righteous power that was *just* inside Patton's grasp will never become mustered again because we've become a nation of simps and grifters who accept their branding as cattle would. Patton was on the cusp of Alexandrian glory and then the *killers* got to him. And when he was rising back from the dead in his hospital bed, they got to him *again.*

Are you angry or are you going to piss your pants and let the rest of us down? Are you going to do some sniveling performative disavowal so you can look good to your other circumcised buddies and the mediocre middle-aged women who also say nothing? We were so close. Let's take it over the top this time. Let *them* piss their pants, for a change. Terrified of another Patton, one not bound by the elite rules all higher officers are beholden to. The spooks reading this book will put me on some corkboard, thinking I want power, jumping to conclusions about what Patton would have done. I want the truth, you bureaucratic simps. I want peace on Earth, you sheep droppings. You think I'm anti-Semitic? I think *you* are anti-Semitic. I actually give a damn. I actually broker peace and put people together. You drive everyone and everything apart.

High School

If I had to give the valedictorian speech for my high school graduating class of 2004, I would say something like this:

Dear Graduating Classmates of 2004,

Phew! Glad we weren't gunned down by a school shooter or blown up by Al-Qaeda! By the way, Mr. Oleson, you're a boring but competent principal. The last guy we had in here turned his daughter into a lesbo and we had to deal with her getting a bunch of unearned attention the last few years. What else, well, our soccer team consisting of 12 sturdy Mexicans and a white guy won the state soccer championship last year. That was impressive! The quality of our Mexican stock will deteriorate in the years to come as the more illiterate and less sturdy Mexicans further south in Oregon begin their migration northward on account of the medical marijuana industry taking off. This was our peak Mexican year. They'll start to be a nuisance in about five years and then in about ten years people will start pulling their kids out of the middle schools and high school in order to put them in private schools.

To all the girls I constantly thought about having sex with in order to cope with the sheer boredom of being trapped in classrooms helmed by dimwits, I say to you: I can tell which ones of you have nice facial structures and which ones of you have already peaked. You will be surprised to find out that the most excellent of you ladies will not hit the peak of your looks until you're about aged 25. Please, whatever you do, do not squander your lovely genetics. Choose smart dudes with quick reaction times and a competence for providing for family. Don't choose guys outside of your race or even your religion, for that matter. Don't go to college and don't move to a coastal state besides Oregon. I am going to watch many of you get advanced degrees and become unhappy hippy women because Oregon churns out hippies like no other. You have been shielded from the effects of multiculturalism but an economic crash in 2008 will push a bunch of Californians northwards, including a massive Hispanic contingent that will coincide with the aforementioned medical marijuana boom.

Our school is going to hell and that's because America is going to hell. Nothing gets updated anymore besides the roads because people start sending powders to government offices if the potholes get too out of control. Notice our lockers are from the 1980's? That's the last time there was any significant wealth in the United States and everyone back then who was in their prime earning years just engorged the size of government. Reagan was a near total fuckup politically but he was enjoyable to be around as a person. And he kept us out of big wars. Bush is considerably worse. You won't be able to fully distinguish them until a black dude gets tokenized into office by insecure whites seduced by his humble

94

foreign policy. You're going to learn that the civilized world is run by pedophile blackmailers who deep-program mass shootings in order to distract the public from the huge financial swindles they're engaged in.

By the way, that one teacher's assistant who works with all the ESL students because he's a Mexican? Yeah, he's fucking the Mexican girls. Bunches of them. He takes them aside during Saturday School for like a half hour at a time and they come back with faces flushed and sweat on their brows. You'll probably want to lock that guy up. Also, that middle school teacher that got caught a few years back screwing those two blonde and brunette girls? Yeah, he's going to resume his relationship with one of them this summer. And his ex-wife, who is a teacher here, is still so fucked up about it all that she's going to try to seduce one of the boys at our high school. She'll stop short though because she actually wants a grown man. She's got a decent conscience but watch what happens when a few hippy liberal women teachers get hired in about five years. She's going to flip her gourd. She'll do anything she can to fit in with them. The drama teacher that just got fired for being too friendly with the students? Yeah, he's a homosexual pedophile. He's going to hang around town living off of social security. He owns his own house and can afford to just bum around, having sex with whatever wayward teen boys find their way to his house after he's offered them marijuana.

By the way, one of the coolest dudes in town, the guy who owns the local gym, is going to get divorce-raped. His wife is going to run the gym as part of their settlement and she's going to take everything and acclimatize it for women. The gym will go under because it couldn't withstand changing away from 20 years of

95

reputation as being a male space. About five years after that, a corporate gym will pick our town because our population will have gone above a certain threshold. But the corporate gym will suck horribly and everyone will miss Bill's gym. Mario will try to revive it. He's a nice guy but he's not all that smart or personable.

The gym teacher is a homosexual. He's an old school homo, though. He doesn't want to seduce kids and he votes conservative. He's not a bad dude but he should deal with his stuff. The choir teacher is also a homosexual but the bad kind. He's the kind to cockblock teenaged boys because he gets off on them being sexually frustrated. He's a sicko. You guys should fire him but you're not going to. He's going to work here until his wheels fall off. He will top out on the teacher salary, which is somewhere around $70k.

A bit on me: I'm about to make a huge mistake and go to a state university for five years. I'll come out with two, semi useless degrees, and I will leave the country because I'll realize what a shitty mistake I made. The madness I'll uncork will drive me to simply make as much money as I can while I deal with the fact that I'm strapped with massive student loan debt, the economy is in complete shambles, and my generation is full of masturbating chimps and dorkus women who think it's their life's purpose to get advanced degrees and make a play for John Mayer lookalikes at wine bars. Eventually, after enough books read, some good psychotherapy, and a bunch of Internet fights, I will emerge and do some great things that none of you will care a damn about. I'll help tons of people get over awful addictions, find love, get married and have children, and create successful and **ethical** vocations for themselves. A majority of you are going to vote for Hillary Clinton someday. I hear you cheering now. That's because you're idiots who hate the white race. Yes, boo me all you want. You're the ones about to die from heroin, *get huge student loans you can't pay off, have too few children, and move to Portland because blacks haven't quite yet figured out it's a strong economic center. You're the ones who are going to come home for Thanksgiving every year, getting drunk off of Willamette Valley wine and thinking you're hot shit. The smartest ones of you will move to NYC and become homosexuals. The most practical of you will start a local construction business and have five or six kids.*

Here's my advice. Don't watch Chapelle's Show. Enjoy Halo while you can because it's going to suck soon enough. Buy Bitcoin. When we have an African black President after Bush, buy as many houses as you can on the cutthroat deals to be found. Real estate is going to skyrocket for at least a good decade after the economy crashes because, surprise surprise, the Federal government is going to do its damndest to turn America into Pakistan-China. Invest in Amazon. Don't have sex until you're married. There's going to be a lot of sex for a lot of people in the next 8-10 years and really, you're not missing out on much. Don't go into the military unless you want to see your buddies blown up by roadside bombs. The Pentagon audit files got blown up in Building 7. The government will spend about $6.4 trillion on phony wars in Afghanistan and Iraq. Europe is going to hell already, so save up your pennies and go visit it before the Notre Dame burns down (and it will!) Don't jerk off to porn. Accept wage work right now because in 10-15 years they're going to make you sign homosexuality loyalty pledges and expose you to all sorts of degrading office environment stuff that Asian middle managers picked up from their home countries. Don't smoke weed. It makes you more susceptible to the aims of one world government. Also, Jewish people are not white. They're their own separate race and that's okay. They run the media. They run banking but they put *stooges in the CEO positions to throw people off the scent. Buy property near Portland as soon as you can because it will triple in value by 2020. Oh, government planes are going to run chemtrails over our town, starting about two or three years from now. A lot of people are going to get feet neuropathy and have thyroid problems as a result. But the guy who runs the local paper is too stupid to pick up on the pattern and the people who run The Oregonian are in on it. Also, the county government is going to put big green gates up on all the logging roads and nobody will be able to get in and out of the forests around here anymore. Go have your fun in the woods while you can! Lastly, no music that is popular right now will stand the test of time. All of the mainstream music is dogshit and you should stop listening.*

That's it from me. Thanks for little. A couple of you were cool. Most of you are brainwashed. The nicest we ever were to each other was when Jared's father died. Everyone was good to him. It was nice to see that. We all should have been more Christian to each other. We also need to give these Boomers a hard time because they're raging, self-indulgent, narcissistic babies right now and don't understand that exactly 1/3rd of all wealth in the United States is about to be wiped off the books…right when the black dude becomes President. They don't understand that they shouldn't be buying boats, extra cars, and pressuring you guys into going to college. They should be savvy. We should bust their balls a bit.

People Getting Stabbed To Death

London is experiencing a rash of knife violence unseen anywhere else in the developed world, aside from maybe Sweden. We know it's happening because of a confluence of factors, namely:

      A) the government is breeding terrorists

      B) the government is importing Arabs

      C) said Arabs want Sharia

      D) the British media is anti-white

      E) the British government has banned guns

The British Isles are being colonized and white people are not allowed to say anything about it. Same is happening all over the West. This is the main thing that matters right now.

Let's say you're at a shopping mall. A pandemonium breaks out as some 85 IQ Arab dude yells out, "Allahu Akbar!" He's sprinting toward you with a massive butcher knife. Do you run away? You better run faster than him. Or let's say he's right next to you when he decides to attack. He's jabbed you once badly through the shoulder and you're bleeding like a burst watermelon. What do you do?

It's too late. It's too late at this point. Nobody expresses surprise when a London knife terror victim's university thesis is about how too many non-white people are in prison. He has succumbed to the system he is seeking to prop up. He's been simping for the Leviathan and in return, the Leviathan has butchered him in the street. And all day long the lying press depicts straight white people as fascist goose steppers looking to burn down black churches or firebomb gay weddings. Al Pacino has been playing a bloviating Jewish person quite often, as of late. That's the only career option he has left. That's the only role available to an older man in what amounts to a modern-day Weimar Republic: an old Jewish mastermind who assembles an elite, diverse team of 21st century Nazi hunters – including a cigarette smoking lesbian in a Catholic nun's habit. Is this indicative of the true nature of society? Are wealthy old Jewish masterminds using mass migration to wipe…

A secret agent steps in my way and tells me that this is a distasteful section of my book that could just have easily been removed from the book without reducing the value of its content. He shows me his Amazon book sales and asserts that he knows more about authorship than I do. I bend the knee because I have been convinced by tolerant voices that I am paranoid. I trust these voices because they remind me of Mr. Rogers, Bill Nye, Steve Urkel, Tom Brokaw, Tom Hanks, Will Smith, and Oprah. The lights dim slightly in my room. There's a Christmas feeling in the air and I can just barely glimpse the outline of Steven Spielberg gesticulating to his cinematographer from behind a large monitor. Sorry, reader, I only have good mindsets now. The truth is that if you think positive thoughts, then positive things will happen for you. The people around you are a mirror of you. These are some of the deepest secrets in the universe. I am surrounded on all sides by white-flight Californians or by low IQ Hispanics. I guess I am a mirror of them. I only think positively of them because that's how I drive book sales through my affiliate platformers. Phew, okay, the secret agent steps away from me as he is satisfied by this paragraph. He puts his finger to his lips and gives me a mean scowl.

The jihadists! Yes, they are the enemies of Western Civilization. Look how they blow things up. These jerks. Ugh! They are bestial warmakers. They oppose our Judeo-Christian values. As Dennis Prager tells us, it was the Jewish holy text that established the *true* sexual revolution of one man, one woman. The Christians borrowed this edict and helped the Jews out in establishing Western Civilization. But now the mean and nasty Muslims, who have many brides, are throwing gays off of buildings! You know what's worth billions of dollars? Ensuring that gays don't get thrown off of buildings, obviously. Imagine you're a gay guy engaged in a freak-dance with your black boyfriend, Eduardo, on a rooftop where there's a swimming pool and an open bar (free drinks, woohoo!) You and Eduardo are eyeing a mischievous looking and oh-so-delightfully-tan Greek homosexual who has these cherub butt cheeks you can spot under his short shorts. He's obviously down for a threesome. All you have to do is ask. You're about to go over and invite him to your hotel room when -BOOM! - the hinges of the door up to the rooftop detonate into pieces. Men everywhere are screaming in horror. Palestinian Jihadists, carrying a banner of Yasser Arafat, stream into the rooftop club. Lucky for you, this is a nation that respects gun laws even more than the United States does. Eduardo whips out his massive machine gun from behind his back and a loud grinding noise erupts as a stream of bullets splatters all over the bodies of the terrorists just as they're about to throw one of your buddies off the building. All of the terrorists are dead, thanks to your black boyfriend, Eduardo. A cry of victory happens just as the DJ drops the beat and everyone gets back to freak-dancing. Spontaneous chants of, "Char-lie Kirk, Char-lie Kirk," break out and everyone rejoins the festivities.

Today is a special day because there's an LGBTQ hashtag for it on Twitter.

Man Learns Secrets About Women From Man

I am a relationship alchemist. On my website, Mastering Self, I have forty essays, all catalogued numerically despite having actual little concursion. Here is an excerpt from one of my essays:

Because my philosophy is rooted in DNA and Sisyphus Unleashed Methodology, I can only speak to people who are committed to biological reproduction. Therefore, my philosophy addresses the heterosexual orientation exclusively. Thusly, I have nothing to say about any other orientation or lifestyle choice. I have literally no interest in what consenting adults choose to do behind closed doors. I don't want to hear about it.

If you have a problem with that, you need to man-up and match my esteemed philosophical body of knowledge and the best way to do that is to spend at least three hours of your weekend morning reading my website (what only a few noble kings "thus spaken", to borrow a Nietzschean turn of phrase. Impressed? Sign up for the Man Cauldron, a 31-day intensive workout regime and male-only space where we practice the divine alchemy of woman-hypnosis on each other. No topic is off-limits!)

As you can see from my steel-eyed gaze on my Twitter profile picture, I know all about the hard times that are to come. Men who have come before us, and I'm not going to articulate exactly who, have made *hard times*. Hard times create hard men. The future is going to be a hardcore landscape of noble leaders such as Titty Cam Kickboxer or Homosexual Runemaster. You think I'm kidding around, mariner, well let me name some more of the up and coming masters who are going to be actual techno-feudal kings when the blood and bullets become "stochastic" (do you like that word? I read it in some light reading: *Moby Dick*):

-Sexy Lithe Tomcat
-Astrophysicist Poker Boxer
-Cigar Boomer
-Tennis Manboob Philosopher
-Eager-To-Please Clout Chaser
-Powerlifter Racemixer
-$10,000 Business Suit Coach
-Panama Hat Date Rapist
-Scarred Rectal Tract Reformist
-Prim Personal Stylist Man
-Skull Ring Navy Veteran
-Muscle Emoticon Christian
-Muslim Who Likes White Women
-Calm-Voiced Social Security Collector

These are the leaders of our movement and their kingdom is ascendant, you outlaws. You think I learned Father-To-Son Secrets from having Chaos Mind (hyperlink to essay)? No, I learned lessons from my Cigar Father because I had Order Mind (hyperlink to essay). Those Father-To-Son Secrets are my gift to you, Red Pill Soldier (even though I have my objections to Red Pill Philosophy – hyperlink to essay). Carpe diem quid pro quo vice versa. Are you impressed with my mastery of the Latin language, renegade buccaneer of the soul? I bet you had to log in to Google to search for that long sentence I used in an Ancient Language. I didn't have to because I am fluent in the alchemical philosophy. I am an Inheritor of Aristotle.

Did you know I used to be homeless? Yeah, my father taught me a hard lesson about life when I was eighteen by killing himself. He always used to put his hand on my shoulder and say, "Son, someday you are going to inherit all of this" just like Mufasa did with Simba. He would wave his hand across the landscape before he took another puff of his cigar. Ah, old times. They get me misty-eyed. Now when I am doing Mastering Self workshops with small groups of men, I sometimes look way off into the distance and remember that Mufasa Moment. My Mufasa Moments blow the minds of the Midwest clueless white guy engineers and technical workers who bank $70k+ and gravitate to me solely because I behave with more audacity than them. Life has taught me about pain. When you're under incredible pain, like watching your dad commit suicide from eating too much pussy, pain becomes your life teacher. Pain teaches you about Spirit. Spirit is when you have Mastered The Self. I believe God/The Universe (I use these terms casually and interchangeably because pain has wizened me into a nuanced person) puts pain in your path so that you can overcome it. These peons on the Internet attack me but I am an unmovable force. They will never understand the pain of watching your dad choke out on Latina muff and then leaving the room where your dad's dead body lies so you can jump from a three-story building willingly. I did that. And now my e-book has skulls and bullets on the cover. I also have a skull tattoo running down the length of my leg. And I took steroids for several years. And my wife is a Filipina. Oh wait, I don't have a wife yet. That's my Hyperborean Mentor: Gave Away 1,000 E-Books Last Month. He probably knows more about pain than me. He tattooed the book cover of Titty Cam Kickboxer's e-book onto his cheek and got some e-clout from his audacity.

The term "divine feminine" isn't correct. This is because the term is not fully connected to what it means to be a mother. Semantics *do* matter and this is actually no small point. The whole entirety of the Universe/God's *meaning* is actually hidden in this portal of language. Once you move past the problem of the Death Of God inherent to the 19th and 20th centuries, as I have outlined in my essay *From The Desert of Nihilism to the Throne of God/The Universe*, you actually see feminists for what they are: evil.

(Quick commercial break: Have you PIMPED your deadlifts yet? Click this link to learn deadlift secrets your dad should have taught you.)

Feminists took the term "divine feminine" and detached it from mothers. That's because they're stupid bitches who deserve to be slapped in the face and knocked to the ground! Surprised? That's because that was a test. If you laughed at that, you aren't a Knight Of Cerberus (hyperlink to essay). You are at danger of dying from pussy underload and we need to flip that right-side-up into pussy overload. The way you do that is you *marry* the forms of "divine feminine" and "motherhood" back to each other. Practically speaking, you write bait posts on Facebook to lure middle-aged white women with funny bird haircuts into attacking you. Then you point out how they're not being motherly. This makes them flip out and then their sons come look at your Facebook business page. You pretend to level with them about video games until you can successfully convince them to copywrite for your website and make shitty, go-nowhere memes featuring your noble Green Beret style profile picture. This is all within your Locus of Control and is on the higher end of Manhood's Hierarchy of Needs (see how I changed "Maslow's" into "Manhood's"?) See my speech "How To Be Redpilled In A Bluepilled World" to understand how you use verbal persuasion to trap scores of young men in your personal bubble of vanity autism that closely mimics the self-indulgent Boomer Generation's 1970's and 1980's fantasy novel scene. Are you ready for this legerdemain? Did you have to look that word up in the dictionary? Maybe you should learn from me. I know a secret or two. Magic begins with blood!

The Bourgeoisie Bites Back

Trump helmed what amounted to a Middle American revival that has since been coopted almost entirely by neocons, Never Trumpers, grifters, and whatever the latest play for time Fox News can cook up. Unless there's some hidden play Trump brings out in his second term, America can reliably continue its downward drift. Balkanization is the current pipe dream of those who can't cope with the idea of deliberately and consistently confronting Conservative Inc. until it lays mashed into pieces on the ground. The funny thing is that it actually takes a bit of imagination to consider that America will stay intact and everything will just get worse and worse in perpetuity. Though it shouldn't be a surprise because what else have we seen? You, as an American citizen, can't even apprehend illegals at the border without the Feds combing through your every move and destroying you with lawfare.

Before it was taken over by mass organizations stemming from the conception of the "corporation" (which, in turn, was a reflection of government bureaucrats realizing there were no actual consequences to leaving budgets unbalanced), America used to be run by a bourgeoisie. This was a localized middle class whose members tended toward Victorian sensibilities of responsibility, impulse control, timeliness, and personal humility. Their clothes may have been drab but notice how cozy their towering, timber-built homes are compared to the bugboxes that are being devised for us nowadays. The bourgeoisie were small to mid-sized employers who ran enterprises overseeing local manufacturing or resource development. The willingness of businessmen to form corporations in order to limit liability on massive loans from the bank in order to outcompete the more austere local employers by making the investment in mass mechanization was what turned America from a bourgeoisie order into a corporate-governmental order. The international bankers, who set down roots in the United States in the late 1800's, had access to such incredible sums that their subsequent loan to corporations had a "fast forwarding" effect that at first, dazzled the Middle American (and continues to dazzle Third World newcomers), but has worn thin as it has become more and more apparent to the bourgeoisie that economic growth for the sake of itself is a road to horrors. Much of the grandeur that old line conservatives place on the 1920's and 1950's can be ascribed to temporal economic circumstances wherein mass organizations rallied strength but not quite past the tipping point of coming at the expense of the Middle American. The lessons of the Great Depression and the 1960's counterculture have not been learned. That these crises are not properly ascribed by the conservative big brains to the excesses of easy credit tells you how little America's intellectual establishment has come to terms with the nature of the problems at hand. In fact, they remain Big Business fetishists on the one hand or climate change psychos on the other. Now the bourgeoisie is biting back.

People are waking up to some hard truths:

-capitalism vs. socialism is a sideshow sold by the Establishment

-Trump is not building the wall

-Congress has as much power as Trump and it is 90% filled with shithead traitors

-America is getting Mexifornicated and big employers have a big hand in it

-Big employers are bringing in Africans, Pakistanis, Indians, and Muslims, by deliberate legal racism, and Trump's Conservative Inc. allies are in on it

-2nd and 3rd generation immigrants don't assimilate

-the non-white favorability polls are slowly inching upward in the face of Herculean efforts on the part of the GOP but *white* favorability has gone down

-record low black female unemployment is touted while whites die off from opioids, drunk illegals, and suicidal loneliness (AKA homesickness in your own country)

-conservative minorities are ethnic narcissists promoted by the Swamp in order to sideline Trump into making good on generations of white guilt instead of making on his mandate

-college is a scam meant to funnel Americans into mass organizations where they are being replaced by cheap visa labor

What's taking place isn't good enough. The people who would be our small-time employers of old, but who instead took out tremendous student loan debt to join the ranks of the bureaucratic elite, are waking up. They're saying, "Hey, Trump, we're still getting the short end of the stick!" The hoopla around the Trump Economy falls flat on the ever-growing contingent of well-to-do's who are starting to notice that we are in a Corporate Economy[2]. The bureaucratic elite are still making out like bandits! The people sick of "the grind" are looking around and starting to make their exit. Turns out that some of that supposedly-cynical jargon from the left on people being "cogs in a machine" is actually true. Turns out people paying mortgages are starting to tire of being accused of anti-capitalist, un-American sentiments for rolling their eyes when they see the stock market hit new highs and corporate kickbacks putting more Teslas into the pockets of Indian word-memorizers. America isn't getting any cozier.

Some of the bourgeoisie isn't content to book it to the hills and live in tasteful tiny homes. Some of the bourgeoisie isn't satisfied to watch Chinese migrants come into the Bay Area to get-rich-quick off of visa schemes dressed up as driverless cab service equity. Some of the bourgeoisie wants the Old Middle Class back. You know who gets rich off of automation? (Yes, the automation that libertarian theorists tell us is a non-issue and that it will free up people to do more human-oriented, artistic work.) Mark Zuckerberg gets rich off of automation. *He* and whatever

---

[2] https://twitter.com/SteveFranssen/status/1140652332188704768

Communist stooges he surrounds himself with get more free time to pursue their autistic endeavors. Jeff Bezos gets rich off automation. Some small portion of the day traders dumping reams of borrowed money onto tech, robotics, and cloud firm stocks will be the ones who suddenly can buy mansions on Seattle's Mercer Island and pretend to be organic farmers. Socialism begets more socialism. The mythical "hard reset" that Austrian economists keep promising us can be kept at bay in perpetuity when even small banks can print money out of thin air[3]. Some of the bourgeoisie will learn from observing the swindles in the Era of Trump (much of it not his fault, to be sure) and will seek other means for righteous, moral societal change. Not only will it be the middle classes who up the stakes, it will also be the people who have been perpetually screwed out of "making it" into the middle class on account of the soaring, fleeting standards for what it means to be middle class. One year it's $45k a year to make. The next it's $50k. Now it's $65k. These people have been wronged. And they won't always turn to Marvel movies and Joe Rogan-esque thinkpieces on the vagaries of Ron Jeremy's sex life or whatever else the culture burps up in a moment of indigestion. These people are going to use the economic means at their disposal to tear down the mass organizations, bloody the nose of the Leviathan, and shirk off the hordes of foreign nation agents. Ironically enough, the scene will be similar to Joker in *The Dark Night* burning a mountain of cash, saying, "It's not about money. It's about sending a message."

---

[3] https://www.sciencedirect.com/science/article/pii/S1057521914001070

Vulture Capitalism

In a recent piece on what is destroying rural America, Fox News host Tucker Carlson took aim at notoriously litigious billionaire hedge fund manager and political financier Paul Singer (no relation to alleged pedophile Bryan Singer). In the segment, Tucker says:

> "[T]he model is ruthless economic efficiency: Buy a distressed company, outsource the jobs, liquidate the valuable assets, fire middle management, and once the smoke has cleared, dump what remains to the highest bidder, often in Asia. It has happened around the country. It has made a small number of people phenomenally rich. One of them is a New York-based hedge fund manager called Paul Singer, who, according to Forbes, has amassed a personal fortune of more than $3 billion."

He compares the philanthropical outings of men such as Andrew Carnegie, J.P. Morgan, and Henry Ford to the hawkish corporateering of the modern-day super wealthy. Whereas the supposed "robber barons" of yore covered the American landscape in conservation tracts, parks, stone libraries, and elevated wages for the American worker – the new super rich focus on cultivating their celebrity in Washington D.C.

No good can come from the economic and demographic fire sale of Middle America. Paul Singer would have to give back the majority of his fortune to make good on the crimes he has committed. Of course, he has been enabled by the Federal government to perform much of it (because of the Fed's garbage trade deals with Asia) but it was *he* who made his choices. No one forced Paul Singer to force the sale of Cabela's (of which he profited $90 million in a week). But it was Paul Singer, who has an army of lawyers, who put the boot to Cabela's neck. This is modern America: a shopping mall dominated by grifters and sociopaths surrounded by squads of lawyers and ultimately, backed up by Federalized police forces. These predators lurk about, keeping whole teams of analysts glued to the markets, and swoop in for a profit irrespective of the cost to Middle American families. These predators have no allegiances to God or to their Fellow Man. They are an internationalist clique that worships money.

What I find especially ugly is that these billionaires are figuring out they need public relations firms to assuage the peasants so there won't be a revolt. And now, not only are these propagandists taking the form of public relations firms, they are posturing as grassroots campus organizations and "think tanks". Where is the "think tank" for the Middle American? There are none because that is not the nature of virtue. Where is the public relations firm for the woman who lost her job at Cabela's and now works at a gas station? It doesn't exist. Where's the nationwide campus organization for forklift drivers who have been squeezed out by Chinese automation? There is none. For too long leftist populists have capitalized on the *real* dissent in America. The Internet is allowing a whole new class of intellectual to form: one who will fight for the average American and who through sheer platform power will bring the giants to their knees. The powers-that-be want to shut down Internet populists because finally there is an intellectual class strong enough to win victories for the American worker. They're trying *so hard* to stamp out the fire that

Donald Trump started but it won't work. We see these predators for what they are: vulture capitalists.

Before I'm maligned by Randian types who would accuse me of operating under the auspices of the Marxist "profit motive" talking point, I'll say this: I absolutely have a problem with people making their money dishonestly. We live in a Leviathan economy. I am not expecting everyone I meet to stop working immediately because they're somehow getting kickbacks from corporations or the government. I *am* expecting people to behave more ethically with their voting patterns, spending habits, and whatever other manner of opposing the Leviathan a person can conceive. If Paul Singer was somehow making big waves in populating Congress with traditionalist libertarians, I would tolerate his vampiric shenanigans – but it doesn't work that way, does it? Lies beget lies.

The Federal Butthead Investigators

Two men in suits knock on the door of Cliff, Steve Franssen's neighbor. When Cliff, born 1955, opens his door, they show their badges to him. He signals his willingness to cooperate and they begin to put questions to him.

The taller man of the two men in suits is actually a female-to-male post-op liberal who voted for Bernie Sanders. He got a criminal justice degree from University of Colorado and used Medicaid to cover part of his transition. He asks Cliff, "Mr. Cliff, we are hoping to ascertain something about the nature of your neighbor, Steve Franssen. Are you aware that he is an Internet racist?"

Cliff, a recent transplant to Montana, makes a mental note to affix one of his security cameras in the direction of the Internet racist's house. He responds, "No, sir. I was not aware but now that you mention it…"

The Federal Butthead Investigators lean in, anxious to hear the report.

"I *have* seen him feeding his chickens, sheep, and goats while muttering to himself," Cliff offers.

"Unbelievable," the shorter agent mutters to himself. He is a quarter Jewish, three-quarters Italian exercise bike enthusiast who dutifully watches Netflix and once agitated to be put on the Butthead task force that monitors 4chan. "Steve Franssen mutters to himself? Like, racist things?"

"Once I heard him shout, 'Son of a bitch!' when he stubbed his toe on a rock."

"A micro-aggression," whispers the taller agent to the shorter one. "Mr. Cliff, is that the worst of it?"

"Not at all. Now that you've mentioned he's an Internet racist…I recall that he once put an Ace Hardware flyer in my trash can instead of his own."

"You're saying he's a climate destroyer."

"Yes, and… he once asked me to quiet my barking dog who never shuts the fuck up because no one in Southern California ever expected me to quiet the dog because roosters are more common down there than dogs. Oh, and he sometimes drives 5 MPH over the neighborhood speed limit even though literally anyone with a crossover SUV or Subaru Outback easily drives 20 MPH over the speed limit."

The taller Butthead agent began to urinate his jeans from his pee hole. He broke out into spontaneous convulsions from the horror of what he just heard from Cliff. The shorter agent steeled his companion by placing a hand on his back. The panic had subsided momentarily and the taller agent was able to ask one more question of Cliff.

"Mr. Cliff, we want you to be aware of the full, dangerous nature of Mr. Steve Franssen. Based on what you're telling us, it's far worse than we could have imagined. We need you to work for us as an informant. Will you assist us in our investigation?"

"Yes, please. Anything you ask, I will do it," Cliff motioned to his wife, born 1957, to come embrace him. She sobbed into his chest and lamented that they had made the mistake of moving in next to an Internet racist.

The shorter agent spoke gently, "Mr. and Mrs. Cliff, so you are aware – Mr. Steve Franssen may try some extremely dangerous maneuvers. He may try to convince people to stop voting for leftist politicians —"

"Why, oh why?!" Mrs. Cliff screamed. Her small dog, Rat, bounded up to her as he was dismayed by her discomfort. She scooped him up in her arms and once again Mr. Cliff embraced her.

"I understand your pain," said the larger, taller Butthead investigator in his signature high-pitched voice. "He may also give a speech in a major liberal city or have an online debate with

115

someone who annoys him. I can see how this upsets you. Trust me, this guy would shatter all that we hold dear. Luckily, we have an unlimited budget, agents trained extensively in firearms who have personal, political vendettas that sometimes cloud their judgment, and a judicial system that is filled with middle-aged women trained since birth to be terrified of any expressions of masculinity they can't immediately shout down with feminist rhetoric. Fear not, Mr. and Mrs. Cliff. Actually, be very afraid."

They left their business cards with Mr. Cliff and he shut the door. The fright he had experienced caused him to open a bottle of prescription pain killers and down one more pill than he was allotted on the daily. He went to his closet where he kept a handgun and pondered shooting himself. His wife tiptoed into their bedroom and her sobs renewed when she saw him holding the handgun. This was the worst experience of their lives.

Women's Many Accomplishments

What follows in an incredible list of all of the things women have accomplished for the good of mankind:

-give birth to and raise children

-be immigration patriots

Women In Law Enforcement

Here I am, in my study, carefully reviewing video after video of women botching their jobs as law enforcement officers. I am watching them fail to keep their tempers, fail to impose their will on the situation at hand, and be utterly overwhelmed by physical force from perpetrators much larger and quicker than they are. On this current video I am watching, I see a woman officer be a total bitch to a middle-aged lady who is trying to protect her disturbed, grown son. The bitchy officer puts her hands on the middle-aged mother. This upsets the son and he pushes the bitchy officer away. The bitchy officer discharges her gun at the guy, clearly because she doesn't like the foul language he is using and because she harbors hatred in her heart for mentally disturbed men like him. She shoots the mother with this errant shot, of course. Then she tussles with the adult son a while longer, getting her ass handed to her when he's mostly just struggling like an autistic person does when they're having a fit. Now she's on the floor. The grown son is pointing a finger at her, telling her she *does not* hurt his mother. A male officer bursts in the front door and kicks the disturbed guy in the face because America is becoming a Third World shithole and officers can no longer afford the luxury of a moment's consideration as to whether these are Actual Americans that are on the scene or low impulse control, mega violence Equatorials. The grown son is subdued and the middle-aged mother is bleeding out on the couch. Great job, Miss Officer!

Colleges are now doing away with SAT requirements in order to boost diversity. The valedictorian of a high school in Detroit is now struggling with basic math in college. How long until a female officer accidentally shoots him after provoking him with ear-shattering screeches to, "Calm down"? How many millions of dollars will the court system then churn through so that someone in this equation can get social justice? Who profits from all this? Why do we heap praise upon these people instead of chasing them out of organized society? Many questions!

The solution is to have all-female police forces. And we should start with the absolute most rural towns of America, make those the first places we have all-female police forces. Why? Because rural places in America are mostly white and white men need to pay the price by having all of their women systematically taken from them and put into the "workforce". When these women inevitably shoot someone to death over some standoff that would be easily handled by a white male, we can just shrug our shoulders because what does one less white woman in the world mean to us? This is the logic. This is the malice of the official decisionmakers. You think that the bigwigs are "victims of brainwashing"? Clearly you don't see the bloodlust in their smiles. Don't you see it? When they go and meet with Trump, they smile in this certain way that you'd think would be indistinguishable from the affect they experience when they're at their blood orgies. You have to go to a vacant, happy place when you're undergoing the humiliation rituals you're subjected to before you can join the official decisionmaker club. This is the guiding hand of workplace diversity. You see a female officer failing to control the situation. I see Satan.

A Woman's Place

A woman should be supporting virtuous men who fight the moral battles of the day. That and she ought to be having children. That's all that is required. There's all this pressure for women to be more than they are. What a sin. The greatest women alive today are either outright immigration patriots or they are the wives of immigration patriots, working on the home front. That's all there is to it. There's no need for a woman to get in with foreign mobsters, weaponize her chest against simps, go into space as a lesbian would, or even "fight foreign propaganda". All a woman needs to do is love a good man and pick up a rifle and fire in the direction of the gates left open to the barbarian hordes. The West is under siege. Have you forgotten about the siege? So busy tracking secret agents that you forgot about the loud brawl at the walls and at the gate? There's a death struggle and the graveyard spreads. What better can women do than to be fertile and to fire in the right direction, if they're firing at all?

You think I'm against women? You think I harbor resentment against them? What a notion. We're all prey to the culture of dysgenesis and dilution. Why would I get real upset with women? That gives them more power than they know what to do with. That's giving them a mech suit armed with chain guns when there are plenty of rifles lying on the ground. I love that scene from Mel Gibson's Vietnam war film *We Were Soldiers* where Sam Elliot's character is prompted, "Maybe you oughta get yourself that M-16." He responds in his trademark grizzled voice, "Time comes I need one, sir, there'll be plenty of em' lying on the ground." There's plenty of rifles lying on the ground. Why make a show and scene about it by arguing with a woman and expecting some kind of validation from her by sperging out into male-female relations talks? There's a fuckin' war going on and I'm supposed make a sales pitch to women? By the way, you can skip all the women scenes in *We Were Soldiers* and the film is even better. Same goes for all of the Joaquin Phoenix scenes in *Gladiator*, by the way. Try it.

Good women know what to do. Good women also influence other women into being good. But women should not be distracting men, pulling money and attention from them. That is wrong. I have no qualms with Michelle Malkin or Ann Coulter in the slightest because they have been firing in the right direction the entire time. And they have no ego in the fight, so they're not a distraction to anyone else. And they've fought harder and better than most "men" in the Beltway. Let's make no mistake, these are high IQ people with intellectual pedigrees. How many "trad" ladies out there don't have anywhere near the knowledge base necessary and are just fouling up the situation for the men we need to be setting into motion? I'd say a great many. You either rock with the best or you turn to your man and provide him support.

We're Attracting Tech Talent!

I have major respect for red-pilled dudes who work as software, cloud, backend, or data engineers in IT. Front end dudes are alright, too, but they tend to be more squirrely, despite being red-pilled. They're a little more susceptible to the poz, you could say. Tech kings *build* systems. They master languages and build with languages. That's super cool. When these guys have done the personal work not to be simps or bugmen, they tend to be highly enjoyable to be around. That's been my experience. Though I can't code much, a lot of what I do has major overlap with what based coders do. I'll start with the smaller picture.

In order to do what I do for a living, which is to write books, speak about reality in a philosophical and illuminating manner, and to consult with people privately, I have had to learn a bunch of languages. I had to learn HTML in order to simply function as an adult (self-care, Dale Carnegie stuff, metaphysics). I had to learn JavaScript, Java, and PHP in order to interface with others (psychology, philosophy, constitutional psychology, sales). I learned Python, SQL, and Ruby in order to write books and speak with knowledge on a wide variety of topics (literacy, analysis, synthesis, composition, memory recall). These are rough correlations but maybe coders will get it.

I like this term *architect* that gets thrown around Seattle, San Fran, and other bigger tech centers. These are the dudes who devise whole new coding languages and get paid the mega bucks. They're the ones you have to pay tons of money to in order to get mentorship from. I aspire to be an architect. My aim is to synthesize all of these languages I've learned in order to create a new language, one that contributes to a major populist upswelling against international governance and mass legal migration. The only thing is that the major firms (Conservative Inc., Open Borders Inc., DNC, GOP, YouTube, Facebook, Twitter, etc.) are not paying major bounties for the next language (like React or whatever is the hot new thing is). They're actively suppressing aspiring architects such as myself. The going ain't easy. Who uses their legal name to say the things I'm saying? Not many! And to do it artfully, with a win-win outcome in mind, and keeping it funny and fun because nobody wants the morose ghosts of our past to come back into the world? Not many people at all.

There's a tipping point sometime in the next few years. Everyone can feel it. Will we tip toward good or toward evil? How much of it is even in our control? Nobody knows the answers to these two questions. So many of us are searching for answers, trying different approaches, and seeing what sticks. If we go over the brink, I'll calm down on all this stuff. I'll do what Ann Coulter said she would do if Donald Trump lost: try something different in semi-retirement. I'll retire from this grinding culture war. I'll write murder mystery novels, as she said. I'll learn to actually code and help some big firm collect mega data. I'll be "non-racist" and semi-compliant. That's seductive, isn't it? To live on your knees instead of dying on your feet? The Leviathan is one of those open pit meat grinders where skeletons and guts get thrown in and chewed into mush that goes into dog and cat food. The meat grinder has a gravity field. To disable the machine, you have to be near it. And if you're not equipped to resist the gravity field, it sucks you in faster. And it spawns baby meat grinder black holes all over the landscape. You're not supposed to run red lights. You're supposed to blink and smile as the grinder sucks you in and spits you out as dog food. The dogs come and chew you up but you're so anesthetized you can't feel anything anymore. Then you're dogshit on the ground that birds peck through and then you're nothing. You're dirt. Then you're made into dirt cakes because the landscape is a war-torn shithole where all the white people have been murdered in cold blood. Some 70 IQ person with eight children, half of them with distended bellies, puts you into their mouth but at this point you're so dead that the sensation amounts to space dust colliding into other space dust. You get shat out into some plastic river that spawns mutant fish.

122

Is that morose? I just got done eating a big breakfast, deadlifting a decent amount, playing with my kid, and starting out my morning right by posting some funny stuff on Telegram. I'm in a great mood. Are you scared? What's *your* deal? Can't a dude talk about things as they are? How about I put a finger in *your* face the same way you pretend to sidle up to me and say, "Bro, u okay?" That's all that amounts to. You're just putting a finger in someone's face. Should I pull a Joe Biden and nibble your fingers? Will that get the chains moving on your fear of speaking truth to power? What is it going to take? Are you not entertained?

Sociopath Signaling

"Did you see what *Known Grifter* said? This time he **really** pissed me off! What an outrage!" says Impatient Stag.

"Why are you listening to him?" I ask from my undersized leather chair that I'm too much of a curmudgeon to sell at a loss so soon after I bought it.

"Yeah, but he's bad. He's just floats from grift to grift. He's insincere. This is an outrage. Surely, you can see it."

"You're not listening to me. Why are you following him on social media?"

"Look at him. He's important, in my mind. I assign him great importance because he knows how to prey on my insecurities. He uses neurolinguistic programming and posts pictures of himself like he's super attractive when at best he's like a 6.5 out of 10."

"You know he does that to get a rise out of you, right?" I ask. "In olden times, when a person signaled to the rest of the village that he was a sociopath – he would either take the town over via the government or he would get knifed in the chest during some disagreement at the watering hole. Nowadays there's no consequences for being a sociopath. Philosophers are literally going around telling people that their superpower in a post-ethical society is to be able to say things with a lot of certainty. These guys are aware of these facts and use it to their advantage. China may be developing a virus to kill all white people but frankly, they don't have to care about that one single bit because all they need to do is grab as much influence and resources as possible. And they have the comfort of knowing they won't be ostracized because Big Tech is operating on the same principles. I'll ask you again, why are you listening to him?"

Impatient Stag considers my question for a moment and then says, "Steve, I'll listen to you. You are the most important because you pointed this out to me about *Known Grifter*."

I say, "Look, people declare themselves all the time. Some guys have a pit in their hearts that they only know to fill with money. They have such a death strangle on the idea that they're going to be wealthy one day that they're willing to manipulate as many people as possible in order to get there. They do this out of insecurity. They consciously provoke envy in other people because it brings attention to them in a way they can monetize. This is completely outside the realm of love. Nor is love some kind of Communist thing where we need to have an Economy of Love or some other madness. But people have forgotten the Blood of Christ. They sell their souls. The only way to buy a soul back is with the Precious Blood."

"I don't like how you're pushing me away."

"I'm not pushing you away. I'm simply bringing your awareness to how much space you take up, how tremendous you are."

"I will kneel to you, Steven! You are so kind to me."

"I don't want your fealty. Help me support my family, that's all."

"You're not going to hawk one of your books to me, are you?"

I laugh and respond, "No! My books don't need hawking. I don't need to self-promote, despite the advice that every person wealthier than me has given to me unendingly for the past decade or so."

"What do you want from me? Tell me what to do!"

"Be true to God."

"Is that the same as 'be true to yourself'?"

"Roughly but there's too many shithead, *Known Grifters* out there who confuse the Self with whatever quiet secrets about themselves that they've buried way under and would need months if not years to uncover through a self-reflective grieving process. Never underestimate the intellect's capacity for self-deception and how seductive a compelling self-deception is to others when marketed properly."

"I guess I don't need to worry about them."

"No, you don't."

Mid Century

Remember when foreign cultures seemed exotic and alluring? Young lovers would honeymoon somewhere faraway, paying for plane tickets that would amount to $2500 in modern dollars. Resorts were still a fledgling industry. Alcoholic beverage makers were in cutthroat competition with one another to establish distribution lines into the Third World. The average man owned a business suit. The average man could afford a leather briefcase and not guard against it being ripped out of his hands by young, fatherless youth. The music of the era, such as Les Baxter or Henry Mancini, borrowed from these foreign cultures but only just a bit – just enough to set the mood. The focus was always on the cozy string sections but you'd get a bit of foreign percussion tossed in, especially the vibra-slap, congas, or the guiro. Americans before 1965 were at an easy peace with the rest of the world (China and USSR non-excepting). Before the inundation, there was something so beautiful happening in our society. Our culture was self-asserting. Yes, I know the toxic seeds of cultural Marxism were already well in-place via the neurotic foreign element in the universities. At the time, had we gotten a whoever-ends-up-being-better-than-Trump instead of Nixon, we could have saved ourselves these past 60 years of unending agony. I call it Forever Punishment. I almost named this book "Forever Punished."

Don't forget: the Third World was once filled with an intellectual elite. Everyone constantly points to the picture of Iranian women before radical clerics took over. Much light is shed upon the women walking around in relatively tasteful garments with smiles on their faces. After the radical clerics? They're all in their black sheets, whatever those things are called. Remember, there was an intellectual elite endemic to these nations that helmed the post-industrial reforms that the West was broadcasting into the rest of the world. Think of how fabulously wealthy and *stable* the rest of the world would have been for the last 60 years if America hadn't completely opened its borders and let the neurotic Neocons run wild... Think of the crossovers that would be happening. The Third World elite were *starting* to borrow from Western culture, incorporating string sections into their clap and conga songs, stuff like this. Listen to Greek pop from the 1970's. Listen to Greek pop from today. These are two entirely separate cultural universes. Medical professionals were being sent from their home countries to train in the UK and America and then they'd *go home.*

Japan, Germany, and maybe Italy had the raw IQ to recover from WWII and build big, technical societies. These nations have even been able to afford bleeding off their more intellectual elite classes to American migration but the rest of the world has not been so fortunate. When you think about it long enough, you realize that the 1965 and 1990 Immigration Acts have been declarations of war on the rest of the world. Come and join us in our white guilt misery! Come join us in our neurotic, vulgar consumerism! The *grown-ups* didn't viciously quell the Hippy Revolution like they should have and now the gold American standard is being bullied by black and Hispanic kids while doddering around on a brain full of Adderall. It didn't have to be this way. It could have been so much more beautiful, orderly, and loving. Remember how everyone wore nice, woolen clothes and sat in the parks the industrialists erected? Do you have any concept of how much cobblestone costs to install and maintain in today's dollars? Remember that pointillist painting from Georges Seurat, showing the common people holding umbrellas, sitting under willow trees, and gazing out into the River Seine. We all got along so well then. Even the criminals were organized and had codes of honor. Now we have the Hmong and MS-13 lurking about, ready and willing to behead anyone in the middle of the night for the smallest of debts. The jungle gyms used to be 10 and 20 feet high. You could break a leg as a kid if you fell! Now everything is Chinese plastic and designed to minimize liability for manufacturers because our society is crawling with lawyers. Coonskin caps, which were en vogue with kids in the 1950's, wouldn't today fly because:

A) There are too many people in America now and such a craze would literally lead to the extinction of the North American racoon.

B) There would be no cultural consensus on what to do with coonskins because the Nigerians would use the skins to stretch onto drums, the Mexicans would make boots out of them, the Pakistanis would make them into baskets, the Indians would lob rotted coonskins over the walls of their Pakistani neighbors, the Italians would make scarves out of them, the Chinese would boil the racoons alive and make everyone barf in horror, and the blacks would make expensive sneakers out of the skins.

We used to be able to make light of our differences without being accused of supremacy. That's because we were mostly similar and because government was much smaller. And because the homosexuals were still in the closet (and they should go back there where they belong!)

Africans are proximal to other Africans. They should all be in Africa where the smartest of them can propagate the glorious, sunny culture of Africa. Asians should be with other Asians, sharing their racial hatred of each other where there's some balance in the eco-system instead of getting into blood feuds with the descendants of American slaves and clogging up our roadways with their women. Russian Jews should all be back together in the seedy, second world villages where they are enlivened to drink and folk dance because of the blistering cold. Americans are the people who sample a wee bit from the rest of the world, not the people who are so inundated and overwhelmed by the rest of the world that they start killing themselves with Chinese opioids at a higher clip than U.S. soldiers died in Vietnam War. You betcha there's a race war going on right now and it is against whites. And the whites didn't police their rebels in the 1960's, so a significant share of the blame *does* go to them. We're 60 years after the fact here so let's see what we can wrangle. Let's bring the coziness back by having a strong cultural base that outsiders have to push up against.

That Which Is Sacred

People are eager to exploit themselves to get social media points. I have never been tempted to do this. The most sacred moments of my life I have never shared over the Internet. I have never spoken about them in a public forum. Let's not be confused, either. I'm not talking about secrets. I'm talking about beautiful, true moments that have defined who I am. I hold those experiences close to the heart. I shroud them in privacy. I do this because I have seen what happens to those who do share them openly: they lose touch. The reason isn't entirely clear to me. There's something in there about public declarations of love. When someone declares their love publicly, they're cheapening it. They turn it into a bit of data for the cloud machines that will rule us all one day. They're doing it for positioning. All you need to do with a person you love is see them in person and look into their eyes and say it. Saying it over the Internet, *especially* in a public forum meant to be seen by others, is cheapening. I don't think there's much wrong with publicly praising a person. *Love* is an entirely separate category. That gets at the divine. I may even say offhand, "I love cookies" or something to this effect but I am not getting at something beautiful in saying that.

Another thing, the artists who have created the most beauty in this life (many of them being those who I have gravitated toward) let the artistry speak for itself. This is why I am not big into self-promotion. I know it sells books, music, etc. I know that I could triple or quadruple my sales (and thus support my family better) by posting links every day to my books and being insistent with people. I see what effect this has on men who become big time salesmen of their own works. They lose focus on the craft, if they had any to begin with, and they join the commercial extravaganza that America has become. I don't want to be like them. I want to be a pure practitioner, like Jesus was. Will this attitude doom me to obscurity? I don't think so. I aim to be so masterful that one day I will become irresistible. I will have used little to no marketing hints. That's the way America was before the 20th century. There was much less advertising, especially when we go back before the industrial revolution. But this reluctance on the part of Christian men to visually and psychically mine the information space for profits was at the heart of some of the greatest works that persisted until just a bit past WWII. Since then, there have only been a few great masters. I could count them on two hands. Maybe three. I want to join that company. The road is severe and I have seen great geniuses walk it and step off of it from the agony of carrying forth. I pray that I won't but it's not a preoccupation for me.

There is more you say by what you don't say. Living this way takes an incredible amount of self-control, especially the more you put out there. This will have been my fourth full-length book in a calendar year. There is a tremendous amount I haven't said and much of it, I have deliberately not said. I keep much sacred because that was the ethic taught to me and because I see it is what has yielded the most intense beauty. I trust the plan. I trust that which is sacred. That is why I will never try to mine profits from it. You will not get it out of me for a price, even if you hire me to dive deep with you like Virgil did with Dante. I will never reveal it yet it is everywhere.

Those Who Heckle Beauty

I have the deepest contempt for those who heckle beauty. This is because they have enough sight to see that which is beautiful. They have this moment, that defines the rest of their lives, where they can choose to submit to the beauty and be changed by it or they can choose to harm themselves by casting aspersions. It takes a certain amount of courage to even behold beauty. We think of Christians in the Middle Ages, going on weeks long walks in order to visit some Holy Site. Imagine being one of these fellows. Getting all the way there and then heckling. You're done for. You don't recover from that. Especially the longer you continue on in your titanic egoism. You wound yourself every day you live without genuine contrition for what you did. The fact that you even did it in the first place comes to define you forever. I have seen this from people I used to respect and it burns to see them in what they've done to themselves. There are mortal sins. There are things people do to themselves that break their spirits. It's one thing to hurt yourself out of ignorance. It's another to have walked the path to beauty and then spit on it when you've arrived. That is treachery that should be isolated and destroyed. We understand when there's a dog that's bitten too many children and has to be put down. We don't understand that people ruin themselves. We tolerate these people. We put them into office. We let them run the culture. They take down millions with them. We live in a graveyard where little beauty yet flowers. And there are hordes of Instagram tourists sprinting from flower to flower, leaving them stamped and mangled. Beauty is mined for money. Innocence is mined for entertainment. I turn away from this graveyard. I always have. I have always known.

Look around you. You see houses going up everywhere yet the median age of white Americans is 58. This is a graveyard society run by hecklers, rapists, and child murderers. The spiritual murder of children has been commoditized and thereafter defended by the "champions of capitalism" who work in towering offices on the coast. Christian families are inundated. You drive to the most rural place in the contiguous 48 and there will still be a hip-hop or pop-country music radio station blasting death into the skies. There is a hunt taking place. Beauty is being hunted down. No stone will be left unturned by the ghouls and imps of the Leviathan. In a video game, you would shoot them with a shotgun. You would tap your flashlight against your leg as the battery dies, hoping to get a few more minutes so you could shoot them as they come to you. It's not only ghouls and imps but those who *know* beauty when they see it and then persecute you with their lies and withering awareness. They pull you in after they've done their mocking ritual. They try their best to set you off-course with distractions, plays for time, long stories about themselves, whatever it will take to pull you off track. They have the scent on you. They know to keep their enemies closer. You know of the beauty they once glimpsed and they don't want you to actually have it. They want you to join their club of doom. They will monitor you…or the most sophisticated ones will deliberately ignore you in order to entice you into pursuing them and stepping off the path. They will act as if you are a person who needs a bit of enlightenment. They'll somehow convince you that living clean is an impossible standard, by whatever verbal trick will work. They'll say you're "purity spiraling" because they can't own how they've destroyed their own brains and nervous systems through misuse.

No celebrity, power, money, sex, or indulgence is worth the cost of beauty. The ones running the show know this and so they take the most genetically beautiful and run them down like hogs. They make elaborate, supremely expensive rituals out of ruining the genetically gifted. You will constantly hear about the genetically beautiful. You will know every passage in their rituals, if only you are listening closely. Whole "careers" on display that simply serve as a warning: if you oppose us, we will ruin you by every conceivable means until you submit. All around you are graveyard dwellers who funnel you to the great vampires helming the mass organizations. "Go toward the light," they lie and lie. You stay out of mortal danger if you respect beauty, if you never join the ritual. Most people don't even know they bear a brand. They don't know who their master is. Their spirits were killed as children.

Trad Space Lesbians

Liars drape themselves in the vestiges of beauty and God. We're meant to think that lesbians in space is a good thing but look at how the first space lesbian defrauded her legal spouse back home on Earth. That's the way it will always be with these people. They're leopards that can't change their spots. Every time they're somehow granted a new horizon by the old guard, they fucker it up. I talked to a space lesbian once at a gathering. I reached out my hand to greet her and then realized you're not supposed to shake hands with women. How tricky of you, space lesbian! That's the unsettling effect these space lesbians have. Combine this effect with the fact that the more sophisticated of them talk about traditional values and suddenly you can't tell your left from your right.

Remember, they're draped in the vestiges of moral legitimacy. The fact that they sow confusion wherever they go is simply their performative advantage. They're operating deep within the leftist logic while putting on a show, convincing you they're made of *The Right Stuff*.

You say to me, Steve – those space lesbians aren't so bad. I'm willing to entertain the thought. In the meanwhile, I say to you, look at the opportunity cost. Who else could you be interacting with? Did you forget about the farmer or the rancher? Did you forget about the local hardware store owner? Instead, you're lavishing this trad space lesbian with attention. They're savvy with the modern means of communication and you can't think to yourself that maybe a less verbose, more paced mode of verbal interaction might be more substantive. You're caught up in the glitz and glamour of the trad space lesbian. But the space lesbian will always defraud. She knows she doesn't belong in space. She won't let that go. You'd have to kill her before she let that go. The secret is that she's killing herself. She doesn't want you to see it. She wants to give her speeches on how she knows the way back to decency but then when people's backs are turned, she defrauds the people in her personal life. She deals in gossip and intel. That's what it takes to be a lesbian astronaut. You think she got to space by the power of her own doing. You're mistaken. Lesbians don't belong in space. We know it to be true. Doesn't mean they won't make it to space one day. It means that they aren't the pioneers they pretend to be. Lesbians make it to space because of the actual guys who are made of *The Right Stuff*. Everyone who follows in their wake needs to give them their due. Space lesbians don't do that. They detach with tanks full of bullshit and when they pierce the cloud cover, they trumpet loudly to everyone back on Earth how they themselves of their own merit did what they did. No spectacle could be more boring. Yet, here comes Hollywood with the biopics.

If you're confronted with a trad space lesbian, and they're everywhere, just remember that just by knowing what you do (from this part of the book) – she will always resent you deep down. She will always subtly undermine. Some trad space lesbians (traditionally referred to as "butch") will harangue you openly in front of your companions and coworkers. Their kind is receding because of the soylent nature of the American diet. Their culture is gone because the farmers and ranchers have mostly sold out to stay afloat. No more hardy-hog butch brawlers to smashmouth their views into the stratosphere. No, all we're left with is the newer variant: the trad space lesbian. Funny to think that lesbianism has seen an evolution. What weird times we live in. If you've never been in contact with a trad space lesbian, that's probably because you've never lived in a city with over 75k people. They are drawn to coolie-density because that's their launching pad. You need a certain amount of concentrated liberalism to fill your fuel tank up with bullshit. You need a certain amount of overlay between mass organizations to lap up the false acclaim that is bestowed on the space-faring lesbian. Hey, do you at least play video games? Trad space lesbians can be seen there. Play *The Outer Worlds* for a minute. You'll meet more than a few. They are the new man. A rare few of them are self-aware but unrepentant. All of them will dislodge you, however. They're fraudsters! That's their nature.

Our society can't even agree on who should be sent to space. We're too busy dealing with the multiracial dystopia. Space lesbians see themselves as volunteering courageously into the fray. Their ambition is uniquely strange. All it takes to shoot them down

136

is an awareness of their nature. But don't think they wouldn't hunt you down like a dog if they could. They're with the secret agents, deep down, the Subverters I was mentioning earlier. They trample beauty just like most everyone else. Don't idealize the trad space lesbians! Don't give them decision-making power! Cajole them back to Earth and put them in kitchens where they can cook and clean. Never underestimate the intellect-run-amok of a space lesbo. Never underestimate her ambition. Make her peel a whole room full of potatoes, like Donald Duck was made to. The discontented need to peel potatoes, not organize and lead our societies! Go to Washington D.C. and witness all the space lesbians running everything. You'd be surprised at how few straight people there are in the halls of power anymore. Even the straight dudes are drawn there by the allure of staffer muff. And the old dudes are corrupted and openly celebrate space lesbians. It's a queer world. You're not supposed to criticize any of it. You know who's in power by figuring out who you're not supposed to question or criticize ever. It's the space lesbians, time vampires, secret agents, corrupted beauty seers, and bankers who are in charge. The space lesbians are the S.S. of the Establishment. They are the vanguard of the Establishment's ambitions.

We understand when we are shown depictions of beautiful women being seduced into working as secret service agents. *La Femme Nikita.* Do we understand the intellectual vanguard that has arisen from the easy sex of mass organizations? We'll need to if we're to recall them back to Earth so they stop pulling huge amounts of attention to the wrong ideas. How do you persuade secret agents to stop butchering Middle America to death? We're going to need some pretty incredible verbal skills to do that. It goes beyond artful arguments and into the sheer cacophony of everyone screaming for attention. How do you artfully dance your way through all this so the space lesbians are disabled and peeling potatoes? We have the answers. We have to dig deep. Same goes for the bankers and all the other dickheads I've taken aim at in this book. I'm not saying there's no redemption for anyone and so we should just start swinging the axe. What I am saying is that we first need to fully deal with the very real possibility that none of them can be redeemed. That's where we form our position of strength from. Imagine it: none who participated dealing out the Forever Punishment can be redeemed. Not even the middle- and lower-class dudes who participated in order to turn a buck for their families. Is that unfair? Maybe. But deal with it. Inhabit that perspective. Then you'll start to spot the trad space lesbians. Then you can do something about all of this. Anything less is autistic. Good luck!

The Calculated Approach

We have precisely 20 years before America will reliably vote hard socialist in national election. This is a scientific fact! We have 25 years until non-Hispanic whites are a minority. Texas is perhaps 6 to 8 years out from flipping blue, based on current trends.

One wing of the conservative movement has an interesting and even a bit romantic notion of what to do: shift the black vote to the right by 4 to 6% to ensure Republicans can win elections. Let's throw aside the hard evidence of Hispanics voting hard left and their guarantee of *double* the population of blacks come 2045. Let's ignore that "Asians" and Hispanics are outproducing the African American community and that Africans vote harder left than their slavery-descended brethren. Suddenly, it's an interesting gambit by conservatives. Suddenly, all of the brash tokenism and celebration of lowered standards makes rhetorical sense. However, that is not reality. That is a play for time out of fear of being called racist for making direct appeals to white America (the only population in the world that overwhelmingly supports gun rights).

A calculated approach may be to bear the brunt of significant losses in the short to mid-term, politically speaking, in order to place our people into positions just in time for America's curtain call. Perhaps we have to grant the endlessly wealthy dotards their Pyrrhic victories while we put our crack commandos into position. I have seen too many American populists gunned down when they jumped the gun. I have seen too many genuine reformists diluted and eventually picked apart by minds more Machiavellian than themselves. What if we make a play for exactly 20 years? We let the losses ride and our noses get nice and bloodied. What if the only shot we have left is a puncher's chance? Then the game changes, doesn't it? At least for some of us. At least for those who have 20 years of patience while Texas flips blue and the GOP starts to host hip-hop awards ceremonies. Isn't there less desperation for us in this scenario? We get to have more focus. We concentrate on final victory while allowing the grifters their grift, the vain intellectuals their self-indulgence, and the foreign out-groups their chauvinism. We don't *have* to purity spiral, shit test, or require total coherence from our allies. We're not in End Days yet. We have 20 years to go. It's not going to be a walk in the park. It's going to be punishment. Socialism spread like a plague. Taxes will soar. But our play will still be in motion. I'm not talking about a coup. What the hell? I'm talking about cultural victory. I'm talking about winning the argument and then assuring the argument will always ring out loud and clear. You won't have to dig around some hidden library in the basement of a crusty castle to find the one moth-bitten tome about all of this stuff. That's the world I'm living for. I might talk some shit but hey, I want *everyone* to succeed. It's in *everyone's* best interests that our people bring home the victory. Only corrupt people win via the Leviathan. I yearn for that end-of-the-day scenario where we dust ourselves off, have a good turkey meal, and pass out on the couch while the kids play. These are family values I've been talking about here in *Coom Consume Comply*. You know I'm not the bad things you've been trained to think. I may have cussed but did I curse someone? Are we cursed, is our fate decided, or can we blow open the whole thing one more time? It's been a long time since 1776. I think we can. I'm optimistic. We can close down what the Leviathan is doing and sort ourselves out. I don't say this as some positivistic mantra that I hope will come to pass because I spoke it. I say it because I see the path. Others do, too. They see the beauty of what could come. They're the only people I let near me!

Enjoy this book?

Help it gain traction by leaving a review on Amazon and Goodreads.

Made in the USA
Middletown, DE
06 April 2021